C000066094

CAN I TELL YO

ABOUT THE AUTHOR

Mark Pritchard was born in Trinidad, West Indies and went on his first bike ride when he was three years old. That marked the beginning of a lifelong journey pedalling everywhere he could. As a teenager in the early 1970s he discovered the joys of long-distance cycling and the freedom a bicycle could provide. Nowadays he rides around 15,000 miles each year on his family of Bianchi bicycles. The stories of many of his rides in the UK and Europe were told in his first book, *Passione Celeste: Captain Century's Bianchi Bicycle Diaries*. When he is not riding his bicycle, Mark divides his time between Suffolk in the UK and Sacramento in California.

CAN I TELL YOU SOMTHING?

Captain Century's American Bianchi Bicycle Diaries

Mark Pritchard

Copyright © 2020 Mark Pritchard

The moral right of the author has been asserted.

Apart from any fair dealing for the purposes of research or private study, or criticism or review, as permitted under the Copyright, Designs and Patents Act 1988, this publication may only be reproduced, stored or transmitted, in any form or by any means, with the prior permission in writing of the publishers, or in the case of reprographic reproduction in accordance with the terms of licences issued by the Copyright Licensing Agency. Enquiries concerning reproduction outside those terms should be sent to the publishers.

Matador
9 Priory Business Park,
Wistow Road, Kibworth Beauchamp,
Leicestershire. LE8 0RX
Tel: 0116 279 2299
Email: books@troubador.co.uk
Web: www.troubador.co.uk/matador
Twitter: @matadorbooks

ISBN 978 1838592 592

British Library Cataloguing in Publication Data.
A catalogue record for this book is available from the British Library.

Printed and bound by CPI Group (UK) Ltd, Croydon, CR0 4YY

Typeset in 11pt Minion Pro by Troubador Publishing Ltd, Leicester, UK

Matador is an imprint of Troubador Publishing Ltd

For Katherine, Megan and Huw
who are with me wherever I ride.

And for Mary who gave me the greatest gift;
the gift of her love.

CONTENTS

1. GETTING READY FOR THE GET READY

It only took a second; but it seemed to last minutes. Rounding the curve on the bike trail at about 25 miles per hour I could feel my front wheel sliding away. In that moment, that brief second, I knew I was going down. Hard. There was nothing I could do. I remember thinking that I had to fall left side down so that CV remained above me, reducing the risk of serious damage to her. I also remember thinking that if I could lean over into the fall then I might just be fortunate enough to slide into the beach sand at the edge of the tarmac. That would, hopefully, reduce the likelihood of a serious injury to me.

The next thing I knew was that CV and I were lying on the hot sand. My left foot was still clipped into her pedal; my right one had detached itself. After a couple of seconds, I wiggled my toes and my fingers. My main concern now was CV. My beloved CV. Was she intact and rideable? I managed to unclip my left foot and stand up. Picking CV up I was amazed – she was completely undamaged. Not a scratch on her. Phew!

Looking down I could see blood flowing freely from my knee. After wiping it away I realised that I now had three impressive road burns. I must have slid along the tarmac before getting into the sand. I also discovered another bloody burn on my left elbow. Nothing that a few days of soreness, disinfectant and some wound dressings wouldn't cure. I would probably boast some impressive scars around my knee for a few weeks. The hallmarks of a true cyclist! My instincts had served me well. Bike and rider remained intact. No real damage apart from my pride and dignity. "Get over it," my inner voice said.

As I rode back to the hotel, I reflected on how lucky I had been. It could have been game over with either a smashed bike or broken bones or both. And a lucky break for you too because now I've got something to tell you.

After I finished my 2015 tour from Land's End to John O'Groats which I wrote about in my book, *Passione Celeste*, I started to think about what to do next. Two big things happened for me in 2016. First, I celebrated my sixtieth birthday by riding sixty 100-mile or century rides. You can also read about those in *Passione Celeste*. Second, Santa put a USA Road Atlas in my Christmas stocking. I say 'Santa'; I'm pretty sure it was one of my kids. But that's a minor detail. When I started looking through the atlas an idea was born.

Like many people, America has featured throughout my life in many ways. And, like many people, I have never actually been there. American films, books and music have been a rich and regular source of entertainment throughout my life. Growing up in Trinidad, in the West Indies in the 1950s and 60s, meant that American food and television were constant features of daily life. I remember visits to the drive-in cinema where we used to hook up a speaker to the door of our car and watch the latest movie on a very big screen at the other end of a large open-air car park. And talking of cars, in the 1960s an uncle of mine owned a Chevrolet. I can't remember what model it was, but it was massive with huge rear fins and front and rear bench seats that could easily seat four or five people. I have happy memories of visits to the beach with my three cousins and my sister all sitting side by side in the back of the Chevy while the car wallowed around on some rather sketchy tarmac and dirt roads. Hot dogs, hamburgers and popcorn were a regular feature of our diets.

I've learned a bit about American history and have long wanted to learn more about life before 1492 when Columbus discovered the continent. I've since found out that most of the history pre-1492 was handed down through the generations in the form of stories that were told and songs that were sung. Very little of it was written down anywhere and so, sadly, much has been lost. Events post-1492 provided a lot of the focus for my history lessons at school. When I left Trinidad our lessons had reached the start of the 20th century having covered the War of Independence, the colonisation of the west and the Civil War. Amusingly, by the time I came to live in the UK, history lessons there had arrived at the Tudors so I missed out on early Greek and Roman history as well as all that stuff about cakes (Alfred), the sea (Canute) and the Crusades (Richard I).

The sheer size of America, with several time zones, adds another dimension. The huge range of lifestyles, cultures and outlooks might be a bit like the differences here between Cockneys, Geordies, the Scots and the Welsh, but on a much broader and bigger scale. America's place in the world means that it has always featured prominently in the news and other media. The arrival of the Permatan President seems to have given this a new impetus. As a one-time PR person I've learnt to take what I read and hear with a pinch of salt. Fake news – hmm?

This all fascinates me, and I have long wanted to find out more. I thought the best way would be to get on my bike, go for a ride, see some places and meet and talk with a few people. Simples! So in early 2017 I did some research online to see what the options were.

Leaving aside a fully self-supported tour (i.e. panniers, tent, camping and cooking, etc.) there was a range of possibilities for an organised tour. Some companies provided tented accommodation – and some seemed to expect the riders to erect and take down their own tents (no thank you after a long day in the saddle). Others laid on self-catering hostels or dormitory accommodation. Again, no thank you! At the other end of the scale one company even offered a very upmarket, five-star approach and a near pro-racer experience with daily bike cleaning and maintenance included. All with a price tag to match. Nice, but way beyond my budget. Along the way I discovered CrossRoads Cycling Adventures, owned by Tracy Leiner.

Tracy rode her first USA tour in 1995 and has been helping other riders to share and enjoy the experience every year since. Looking at her PR blurb, with my usual pinch of PR salt, I quickly felt a strong resonance. What Tracy described seemed to be exactly what I was looking for in terms of the quality of the ride and the level of support provided. But what really clinched it was the way Tracy described her first ride and how the people on the ride evolved into a team. I felt a strong empathy with my own experiences and aspirations.

My last bit of research was to speak to two UK riders who had done the tour with CrossRoads. They shared a lot of helpful information with me. The clincher though was when I asked them if they would do the tour again with CrossRoads and both responded with a resounding 'YES!' I realised then that the time to stop thinking and dreaming had arrived. On 16 March 2017 I paid my deposit and I was in! Timing meant that I was too late to join the 2017 tour so I had to wait until 2018. But I was going. I was going to ride across America!

Having booked my place I spent the rest of the year getting on with life and following my usual riding programme including a fabulous weekend in North Wales with Team Super 6. We first rode together when we met on the great 2015 Land's End to John O'Groats adventure and we have got together every year since to ride, reminisce and sink a few beers! By the end of the year I had managed to get over 15,000 miles into my legs; albeit with a certain amount of turbo time in my garage when the weather wasn't conducive to road riding.

I had drawn a chart which I kept on the shelf above my desk to count down the days until I left for Los Angeles. The chart started at 'Le Grand Depart' minus 423 days. As I had a good idea of the route we would be following, I spent many hours poring over my road atlas to work out which towns we would be passing through and then trawling the Interweb to find out more about some of the places we would be visiting. All this served to heighten my anticipation for what lay ahead. The tour had the potential to be very exciting; a tough ride but one which I hoped would provide many rewards.

It all got very real early in February 2018 when I sent my final payment for the tour to Tracy at CrossRoads Cycling. Interestingly, within minutes of making the transfer I received a text from my bank asking me to call them. Now, it wasn't what you think. The size of the payment, which I had made in US dollars, had triggered an alert and reassuringly the bank wanted to verify its validity before releasing the funds. I phoned the number and after pushing several keys on my keypad and listening to a succession of recorded messages, I was eventually connected to a human being, a delightful and helpful lady called Josephine. I confirmed my details and she said the payment would be released immediately. She said she couldn't help noticing who the recipient was and asked me what it was for. When I explained, her silence was palpable. Josephine wished me good luck and I said she could follow my progress on my blog. She subsequently sent me a lovely congratulatory email when I returned to the UK. But I mustn't get ahead of myself!

I was now fully committed. There would be no opting out. It was time to focus on completing all my preparations. Bike to be built. Flights to be arranged. Pre- and post-tour hotels to be booked. Insurance policies to be updated. And the small matter of staying fit by riding a lot.

There was a steady flow of emails from CrossRoads in the subsequent weeks covering pretty well very aspect of the pre-tour preparations and logistics. However, one email came as a complete surprise. In early April Tracy announced that she had sold CrossRoads and was retiring! My initial thought was to wonder if I had been the victim of some sort of online scam. I was quickly reassured. CrossRoads was going to live on and, as far as I could tell, was merging with another company, Big Dreams Bike Tours. Interestingly I had come across Big Dreams when I was researching tour operators that I might ride with. I had discounted them at the time because I didn't feel the empathy, the 'wow' factor that I got from Tracy's PR. So, once my heart-rate had returned to its resting state, it was business as usual. Or so I hoped.

While all this was going on, Mick, Sean and Tony at Madgetts Cycles in Diss, my go-to bike store, were building the bike for my adventure. It was very exciting, a bit like gaining a new sibling, or so I imagined. Now, forgive me readers if I get a bit technical here but the bike was going to be critical to my success and enjoyment of the tour. It was going to be my costar in the show. Together I hoped that we would form a long-lasting and loving relationship.

I've discovered that quite a few people who don't ride bikes read my writings, and they contact me if they don't understand what I'm going on about. For their benefit I've tried to be as nontechnical as possible without unduly dumbing down. For the cyclists reading the following words, I know that I risk inviting comment, debate and even argument. We cyclists can talk about components until the cows come home. And then some! The pages of the Interweb are awash with 'expert' opinions. Steel frames, aluminium frames, titanium frames, carbon frames.

Bamboo anyone? One thing I have learnt over the years is that when two riders finally agree on some inconsequental technical detail, one of them is bound to be wrong. So, a disclaimer. Captain Century takes no responsibility for the technical views expressed heirin. They are entirely a matter of personal preference. My preference. Deal with it!

The frame was provided by Bianchi, a company founded in Milan, Italy in 1887 and going strong ever since. The founder, Eduardo Bianchi is one of my heroes and there's a chapter on the company's history in my book, *Passione Celeste*. I've had a long-term love affair with Bianchi so there was no possibility of any other frame getting a look-in. And besides, Bianchi made a frame that was ideally suited to the tour. The frame I selected was a carbon monocoque or one-piece Infinito CV model. 'CV' which is unique to Bianchi frames stands for 'Countervail' which is a layer of vibration cancelling material that is embedded within the carbon layers that make up the frame. Reducing vibration helps to reduce fatigue and muscle stress making long distance riding less tiring. Countervail also enables frames to be stiffer and stronger without increasing their weight. In practical terms what it does is reduce the numbing effect of riding on roads with the wheels vibrating as they roll over the tarmac chips. But make no mistake, if I hit a pothole I was still going feel it. There's nothing you can do about that short of fitting hydraulic suspension and incurring a massive weight penalty. I already owned an earlier model of Infinito, before the addition of the CV technology, so I was interested to discover if the damping effect was really noticeable. (It definitely was as I discovered.)

Normally the groupset (gears, brakes, etc.) that I use is made by another Italian company, Campagnolo. If I'm riding an Italian heritage bike frame then it seems entirely proper to use Italian heritage components. I've been riding with Campag for over forty years and, as the saying goes "if it ain't broke don't fix it". Campag is not that widely available in the USA so if I had to find parts for a repair I might be stuck. Consequently, I crossed over to the dark side and opted for a Japanese Shimano groupset. Shimanono parts, as I call them, are widely available in the USA. The gearing was a Shimanono Ultegra Di2 electric setup which avoided wire cables that stretch and occasionally break. Shifting gears is very easy with light touch fingertip controls. I ran a 50x34 compact chainset – the big rings on the front attached to the pedals – with an 11-30 cassette on the rear wheel. The rear derailleur was a long cage version to accommodate the biggest cog on the rear cassette. In practice what all this meant was that I should be able to complete all the climbs without too much of a struggle, or so I thought. I figured that having more in the tank at the lower end of the gear range was better than having higher gears which would enable me to ride faster. After all this was a tour, not a race.

The finishing kit (handlebars, stem and seat post) were made by Fi'zi:k (try saying it!) an Italian company founded in 1996. Their marketing blurb claims that they strive to make the most sophisticated, inspiring and beautiful gear for the world's most discerning cyclists. Wow! By contrast my pedals were double sided Shimanono touring pedals. Quite heavy, unsophisticated and perhaps even underwhelming. But totally practical because fitting them meant I could wear shoes that I could walk around in rather than my more usual ones which are fitted with nylon cleats that are definitely not made for walking in. The wheels were Mavic Kysrium Discs with aluminium rims. Founded in 1889 at Annecy in France, Mavic's famed yellow and black colours are a well-known sight on the Tour de France. They provide neutral service spare wheels to all the teams in the race. I've used Mavic wheels for over 30 years – the Kysrium range was first produced in 1999 – and this version of the Kysrium was ideal for the sort of conditions I envisaged encountering on the tour. The glossy black rims and thick oversized spokes gave the wheels an attractive yet businesslike appearance. The wheels were shod with my preferred tyres, Michelin Pro 4 Endurances. In my opinion, and I can hear sharp intakes of breath from fellow cyclists, the Michelins strike a happy balance between low rolling resistance, durability, and protection from punctures. On average I get about 3 punctures a year over 15,000 miles of riding on some fairly sketchy roads. If there's one bit of kit that's guaranteed to provoke lively discussion amongst cyclists, it's tyres.

There is one final piece of kit that I must tell you about. Especially as it is probably the most important item. Ensuring that my posterior was going to be comfortable was a no brainer. My saddle and my bum were going to have an intimate relationship throughout the tour and I certainly wasn't going to risk any tension or crankiness in that department! For many years I've ridden Fi'zi:k Aliante Gamma saddles, colour matched to the celeste of my Bianchi frames. Remember their marketing blurb – sophistication, inspiration, beauty? Sadly, I was unable to source a new Aliante saddle with the proper colour combination. Instead I opted for Plan B and went for their Antares R3 model which I'd tried a few months previously and really liked it. Now here's the thing. The Antares is one of the models available under Fi'zi:k's custom build programme and one Thursday evening I went online to their factory in Italy, input my measurements, specified the colour patterns, paid my money and sat back to await delivery which was promised in two to three weeks. Imagine my surprise when, at 10am on the following Tuesday morning I answered a knock on my front door to be greeted by a deliveryman bearing a large Fi'zi:k box! Inside lay a thing of beauty, my new saddle looking and feeling exactly as I hoped. All I needed now was the bike to fit it to.

I'm sorry if I've sent some of you to sleep along the way but this is important information. Trust me. Knowing that my bike was being built was hugely exciting. I couldn't wait to get my hands on it. My patience was rewarded because after a couple of weeks, on 10 April, 29 days before the tour started, I received a call from Mick to say that the build was complete. I hotfooted it over to his store and there she was, my beautiful CV looking exactly as I imagined her. I couldn't wait to take her out for our first ride together. With the saddle fitted I climbed on and was pleased to discover the only adjustment needed was to raise the seat post a few millimetres. The plethora of measurements I had provided for the build was spot on. Everything felt just right.

So, after a celebratory photoshoot with Mick and CV I drove home, donned the lycra and off we went. Our first ride together. I was anticipating a stop-start ride while I made some adjustments. I was totally unprepared for what actually happened. We finished our maiden ride without any stops. Within a few short miles I felt completely at one with CV. It really did seem like we had achieved a magical bond – rider and bike joined together and moving in total harmony. By the time I got home I knew that we were, as the saying goes, "a marriage made in heaven". Over the subsequent days we began getting to know each other. Our third ride was CV's first century and it was a total delight. When we finished, we both felt that we could have kept going and done a double century. Something I haven't done for a very long time. I was delighted, and reassured, that CV seemed to like me as much as I liked her.

Getting CV built and road tested was a major landmark. While all this was happening I had been busy with lots of other pre-tour details, arranging flights to Los Angeles and back from Boston, insurance for me and CV, and hotel accommodation in both cities pre- and post-tour. I planned to spend a few days in Boston at the end of the tour and soak up the fourth of July celebrations. I also acquired a custom-made hard case from a British company, BikeBoxAlan, to transport CV on the outbound and homecoming flights.

One logistical detail had been challenging me. How to get the bike box from LA to Boston and store it there until my arrival? In the end it proved remarkably simple. I found a company called BikeFlights who specialised in shipping bikes around the US. They acted as agents, sorting out all the logistics (i.e. FedEx). Arranging storage in Boston was just as easy. A lovely lady called Teresa Belmonte, who worked for the hotel I would be staying at in Boston told me to get the case shipped to her and she would arrange to store it safely until I arrived. I was struck again by how helpful the people were that I reached out to. Nothing seemed to be too much trouble and most of the people I liaised with went way beyond my expectations. They offered their advice and provided information freely, with great humour and, I sensed, pride. As I was to discover on the road, this level of helpfulness, support and interest was commonplace. We Brits could learn a thing or two from these Americans about customer service.

All this back office stuff filled the hours when CV and I weren't on the road bonding. Much of the rest of my free time was spent poring over my road atlas and Giggling information on the Interweb about the places we would be passing through on the tour. I was filling my notebook with information and getting ever more excited, and a little apprehensive. I also reached out through the global Bianchi network to the Bianchi Owners Club USA – I was already a member of the UK club and became a member of the USA club. I was overwhelmed by the responses I received. Tim Elliott, the USA club co-ordinator was extraordinarily helpful to me prior to the tour and then became a source of encouragement while I was riding it. It seems that the ethos of the Bianchi family really does span the globe.

Although I never met Tim, he felt like a cousin to me. He was a great source of advice and helpful suggestions, always provided with good humour.

As the start date got ever closer I began to think about the other people who I would ride with on the tour. I learnt that there would be one other UK rider, Peter Wilson, from the south of Scotland. We managed to make contact and had a long phone conversation. We discovered that we shared a lot of common interests. Unlike me, Pete had already ridden in the USA as he had family connections there. Pete told me he would be arriving in Los Angeles a few days before the tour started so we agreed to do a couple of rides together. As I put the phone down the omens felt good. Little did I know how strong our friendship was going to become over the coming weeks.

Making sure I had sufficient time to ride while sorting out the logistics was really important. I belong to the Eddy Merckx school of preparation; the key to success being riding miles, lots of miles. As I prepared to leave Britain I had over 5,000 miles in my legs since the start of the year. Disappointingly, a higher proportion than I would ideally have wished had been done on the turbo trainer in my garage reflecting the crap weather we seem to have had. However, in overall terms I was slightly ahead of where I had been at the same time the previous year and I felt pretty fit. The prospect of riding 3,400 miles over 44 days was something I was looking forward to. From the comfort of my armchair at least.

Riding during my last seven days in the UK involved the full spectrum of British weather. The final weekend was wet and cold with, at one point, sleet and hail. I also rode a warm 70 miles in the Fens with Nairo and Richard, two of my cycling friends. If there was one aspect of my preparation that I have missed it was the opportunity to ride in more sunny, hot conditions. With the prospect of crossing the Mojave Desert (30 degree-plus temperatures in the first week) I suspected I could be in for a bit of a roasting. And, disappointingly, my tan lines were rather feeble. I feared that my pasty white legs might provoke some disparaging looks from my fellow riders.

Eventually, 417 days after signing up for the tour it was time to leave. Time to head across the Atlantic to America. On 7 May I woke at 5am and after breakfast and completing a few final household tasks, I loaded the bike box and my holdall into a rental car and drove down to Heathrow. I hate last minute rushes and would rather arrive far too early than be gnashing my teeth as I crawled along the M25 – which has happened before. As it turned out there were no delays and I arrived nearly four hours before departure time! The biggest challenge was finding a petrol station to top up the rental car before I handed it back. It took a mere 15 minutes to deliver the car and get a shuttle bus to Heathrow's Terminal 5. Checking in was effortless; the only delay was getting approval to take some carbon dioxide gas canisters for inflating my tyres. Thankfully, after the check in lady phoned her office I was cleared to put them in my bag to go in the hold.

Once I had checked in and dropped my bag I took the bike box across to the oversized luggage desk. I was the only person there. The attendant looked rather bemused when I asked if he would take a picture of me. But after a bit of negotiation involving the use of the phrases 'riding for my country' and 'riding for charity' he grudgingly obliged. Now at this juncture I just want to let you know that 'my country' was Wales (CV and the bike box are suitably flagged) and the 'charity' was the Green Light Trust. Despite the fact that Terminal 5 was heaving with people flying to all corners of the world, I was through security and into the departure lounge in under five minutes.

The flight left Heathrow on time and somewhere below me in the hold was CV packed in her case. The case comes with a handy little GPS tracker so I was able to confirm CV's presence before I had to set my phone to airplane mode. My first order of business after arriving and, hopefully, a good night's sleep would be to put CV together and take her for a test ride. I had an assortment of tools with me to help with this. After the last few hectic weeks the 11-hour flight provided time to sit back, relax, enjoy the hospitality and try to get some rest. Finally, I was on my way. I was about to have the ride of my life.

After an uneventful flight I arrived at Los Angeles airport at 7pm local time (i.e. 3am UK time). We were swiftly off the plane and in no time at all passing through immigration and customs. After being fingerprinted (both hands) and photographed I got the all important 'admitted' stamp in my passport. Now at this point I should tell you that I breathed a huge sigh of relief. You see, one of my old passports bears a big red stamp in it stating: 'Alien denied entry – carrier to hold pending immediate continuous transit'. On my one previous attempt to enter the USA, aged 11, while flying home to Trinidad in the West Indies with a scheduled overnight stop in New York, I was refused entry because of an administrative cock up.

Once through immigration it was time to retrieve my luggage. My holdall appeared on the carousel pretty quickly and then I made my way over to the oversized luggage point which, when I eventually found it, seemed to be closed for the day. It was completely deserted and although I had been assured that I was definitely in the right place, in my jet lagged state I wasn't completely convinced. Fortunately after about 15 minutes of standing around, the carousel suddenly kicked into life and, joy of joys, out came my bike case. What a relief!

From there it was a quick phone call to Yael the receptionist at my hotel to arrange for a courtesy bus to collect me. She told me that their driver, John, would arrive in about 10 minutes in a black Chevrolet minibus and warned me not to accept any offers of a lift from anyone else. Well, true to her word, John arrived and we loaded the bike case and holdall into the back of the minibus and set off. John was a lovely man and we chatted freely during the short journey to the hotel. He told me that there are 88 cities in Los Angeles County; Los Angeles is just one of the cities. El Segundo, where the hotel was located, was another one. John was almost speechless when I told him that I was going to be riding to Boston. He was fascinated by my bike and asked if he could come and see it before I set off. He also told me that if I wanted a good traffic-free ride to begin with I should try the coast cycle route.

John dropped me at the hotel in El Segundo and Yael quickly checked me in to my large room which had twin double beds and a balcony overlooking the swimming pool. After a quick shower to freshen up I was in bed by 9pm which meant that I had been awake for 21 hours. Fortunately, I managed to get a good night's sleep and when I awoke at 6am I felt completely refreshed. After breakfast in the hotel it was time to unpack and rebuild CV.

I have to say that I was rather apprehensive at what I might find when I opened the bike box but I needn't have worried as everything was still securely fastened. Thirty minutes later I had CV fully assembled and we were ready to ride. So the time had arrived to have my first outing on American tarmac. I packed a few tools in my jersey pocket just in case running adjustments and tweaks were necessary. They weren't. Then, heeding John's advice, I rode down to the coast and on to the cycle path about a mile away which ran alongside the Pacific Ocean, and turned north towards Santa Monica.

Now readers, I have to tell you that this two-lane cycle path was top quality. Smooth surfaces – even the rougher bits, were smoother than I am used to riding on at home. And very popular too with cyclists of all descriptions and all ages as well as lots of people on electric scooters and roller blades. The route gently twisted and curved its way along the coastline and was a real delight to ride. In one or two places sand had blown across the route which made it a bit treacherous for me as I'm not used to riding on sand. With all the new sights to take in I found it quite difficult to concentrate and keep a watchful eye out for the sand traps. The route just seemed to be calling out to me to up the speed. CV was singing as we made our way northwards.

Together, we rode past Venice Beach and Santa Monica Pier to the end of the route just beyond Port Los Angeles Long Wharf about 12 miles in all. After a pause for coffee and a bit of people watching I turned around to head back to the hotel. Ahead of me I could see a couple of riders so I upped the pace and caught up with them. After a while I introduced myself and learnt that Bruce was from Massachusetts whereas Gerry lived locally, just a few minutes away from my hotel. We rode along chatting and they were very interested to hear why I was in California. After a while they peeled off and I carried on alone. It was fascinating to see all that was going on. Beach volleyball was the most popular sport with dozens of courts. It was all quite mesmerising. So mesmerising that I paid the price for not looking where I was going.

It only took a second; but it seemed to last minutes. Rounding the curve on the bike trail at about 25 miles per hour I could feel my front wheel sliding away. In that moment, that brief second, I knew I was going down. Hard. There was nothing I could do. I remember thinking that I had to fall left side down so that CV remained above me, reducing the risk of serious damage to her. I also remember thinking that if I could lean over into the fall then I might just be fortunate enough to slide into the beach sand at the edge of the tarmac. That would, hopefully, reduce the likelihood of a serious injury to me.

The next thing I knew was that CV and I were lying on the hot sand. My left foot was still clipped into her pedal; my right one had detached itself. After a couple of seconds, I wiggled my toes and my fingers. My main concern now was CV. My beloved CV. Was she intact and rideable? I managed to unclip my left foot and stand up. Picking CV up I was amazed – she was completely undamaged. Not a scratch on her. Phew!

Looking down I could see blood flowing freely from my knee. After wiping it away I realised that I now had three impressive road burns. I must have slid along the tarmac before getting into the sand. I also discovered another bloody burn on my left elbow. Nothing that a few days of soreness, disinfectant and a wound dressing wouldn't cure. I would probably boast some impressive scars around my knee for a few weeks. The hallmarks of a true cyclist! My instincts had served me well. Bike and rider remained intact. No real damage apart from my pride and dignity. "Get over it," my inner voice said.

As I rode back to the hotel, I reflected on how lucky I had been. It could have been game over with either a smashed bike or broken bones or both. And a lucky break for you too because now I've got something to tell you.

I'm going for a ride now so why don't you join me. Let's go and have a look at America and meet some Americans…

LOS ANGELES TO FLAGSTAFF : 6 DAYS, 530 MILES

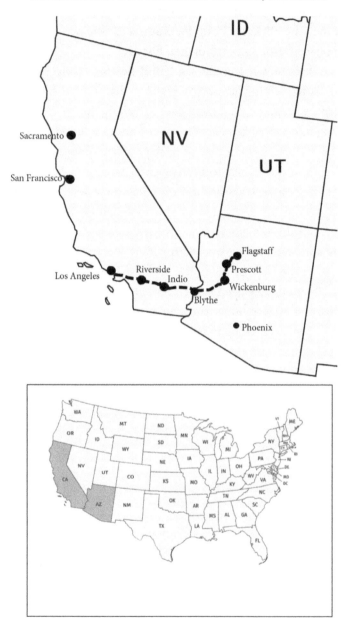

2. FLAGSTAFF HERE WE COME!

Saturday 12 May, Los Angeles

At 4pm I finally met all of my fellow riders and the support crew at the pre-tour briefing session. They were a very diverse group. With the exception of Pete and Emil, who came from Switzerland, everyone else was from the USA. Their ages ranged from early twenties to late seventies. Most were experienced, long-term cyclists; a few have become converts to the cause relatively recently. Some of the riders had already completed the tour in previous years. No pressure on the rest of us then. Most of the group are aiming to ride the whole way from LA to Boston with a small number doing the first third only. And a couple of riders will join us along the way.

All of us seemed to share one thing in common. We wanted to have fun as we rode along. For many of us this was going to be a ride of discovery. A discovery about the places of a great country. A discovery about the people of a great nation. And for all of us I suspect, a discovery about ourselves. Quite a few riders, like me, were riding to raise funds for their charity of choice. Mine is the Green Light Trust, an environmental education charity that supports people with health, lifestyle or learning challenges and helps them to overcome these. If you'd like to know more about their outstanding work look at their website. I have supported Green Light in a variety of ways over the last 30 years – I am currently on their Board as a Trustee. I am donating the proceeds from the sale of this book to Green Light. So, if you've bought it, then I thank you. And if you're reading someone else's copy, come on…!

The support crew all seem very friendly and I already felt a good empathy with them. I chatted to a couple of the crew, Mary and Robin, who were making sure that we all received our packs containing essential information including the daily route cue sheets and an updated contact list. More importantly, they made us feel very welcome. My British accent caught their attention and they wanted to know why I chose to be on this tour. Even at this early stage I got a strong sense that they saw their roles as doing all they could to help us, the riders, achieve the prized EFI status.

This is probably a good time to explain one of the tour's goals. Achieving EFI status is the prize, the holy grail for completing it. EFI stands for 'Every Foot and Inch'. Other interpretations are out there so use your imagination readers! Put simply it means that a rider has pedalled every foot and inch of the way. Walking, and, if you're a purist or being very harsh, walking up part of a steep hill, disqualifies you from achieving EFI status. Freewheeling downhill, I was told, was allowed but I would have to be going over 20 miles per hour. Only kidding! I had to pedal all the way. All 216,000,000 inches of the route from LA to Boston. There's a bit of trivia for you readers. I do like my trivia and I was planning to collect a lot of it as the tour progressed. And if you feel the need to check my calculations, well, do the math yourselves. As we progressed eastwards on the tour, protecting my EFI was always at the back of my mind. It wasn't something that I obsessed about but as the miles added up I became more and more aware of the terminal potential if I had another crash. I am not sure that I altered my riding technique much though!

After completing the introductions and going over some of logistics for the tour we had our bikes inspected for road worthiness (CV barely got a second glance). Then it was time for our first route rap. Route raps enable us to go over the route notes in detail, highlighting any potential hazards and other information such as the availability of food and water on the next day's route.

Following a break to freshen up we all gathered together for dinner before heading to bed for the night to dream about what lay ahead. Those of you who know me will know that I believe a good ride requires a good route. I felt that the omens were good. Achieving a great ride requires great people; riders and support staff. And my initial impressions about the people I would be sharing the tour with were very encouraging. My last thought as I turned out my bedside light was that at last, I was literally on the eve of setting off. I could not wait to get going!

Stage 1: Sunday 13 May, Los Angeles to Riverside (79 Miles)

After a surprisingly good night's sleep I awoke, washed, dressed and by 5:30am was having breakfast with the group. A wide choice of food was on offer and I settled for some orange juice, scrambled eggs and bacon, a bagel with strawberry jam and coffee. I spent a few moments listening in to the tone of the conversations and looking at body language in the breakfast room. I wasn't eavesdropping as such but instead testing temperatures, feeling pulses and trying to assess the mood music. What I heard was lots of laughter and happiness; people who, like me, were ready to ride. Certainly, lots of eagerness to get going but also some hints of uncertainty and even apprehension. For all of us, and I suspect even those who have previously competed what I was about to attempt, nothing was totally certain about what lay ahead over the next 44 days. Each of us was going through our own pre-ride preparations – some quite obviously so; others rather more nonchalantly. For many, including me, we were on the threshold of what might just be the adventure of our lives.

Suitably fuelled up I returned to my room to don the lycra, including the rather lurid tour jersey for today's ride. I also finished packing my bags. We have each been provided with two kitbags and were under strict instructions to ensure that their weight did not exceed 30 pounds. That's in total; not per bag. It was quite a struggle to zip up the bags containing all the kit and caboodle required for a seven-week trip. After a certain amount of shoving and squeezing I was quite satisfied with my efforts and my bags were done up tighter than I thought physically possible. Feeling pleased with myself I had a final look around the room and to my horror I spotted my trainers and a pair of shorts. With a heavy heart I opened up one of the bags and went through the bag stuffing routine again. Eventually I managed to squeeze everything back in and I took both bags down to reception to be loaded into the support van. Then I returned to my room for a few minutes meditation before CV and I left our room at the hotel for a final time.

We were soon ready to set off and we received some final instructions about getting to Manhattan Beach for the official start. We rode the 2-3 miles there in convoy and then it was time for the traditional wheel dipping ceremony in the Pacific Ocean. I picked up a small pebble as a keepsake and put it in my tool bag. Mary, one of the tour crew took an interest in my damaged left knee, even taking some photographs. I may have to keep an eye on her! Once the photocall was complete and with little further fanfare we were underway. Finally, after 423 days since I signed up to do the tour I was rolling. At last, I was on my way to Boston. It almost seemed like an anticlimax after such a long period of anticipation.

We immediately headed due east and inland along a succession of long straight and generally smooth roads. It took a while for smaller groups to form. At the start of any tour riders go through an introductory process as they discover who is similar to them – in terms of riding ability and temperament. Gradually smaller groups formed through a sort of natural selection process. I sensed that my scarred knee hadn't gone unnoticed by some of the other riders who were treating me with caution. Was I the rider who couldn't stay upright? The rider who might bring them down?

The ride out of Los Angeles was through a seemingly never-ending succession of business parks and industrial estates interspersed with small-scale, local shopping areas and low cost, densely packed housing. From what I could see as I rode along it all looked fairly random and unstructured and was quite different from the much more planned approach to urban development that I was familiar with in the UK. It was Mother's Day so on many of the street corners, flower sellers were busy trying to win the attentions of passing motorists. The traffic seemed to ebb and flow as we progressed. We passed over dozens of fourways, crossings where traffic from every direction had to stop and then, following what to me was an unfathomable code, each vehicle moved off in turn. It seemed to happen quite naturally and with good grace. In Britain I suspected that there would be regular outbreaks of road rage if a similar system was used there. Despite the courteous driver behaviour I ensured that I made hard and direct eye contact with any motorist who might cross my path. It amused me to think that back in the UK we have developed our own solution to this situation – roundabouts!

In what seemed like no time at all we arrived at the first SAG (Support and Gear) stop where there was a selection of fruit, drinks and snacks ready and waiting for us. We were required to sign in and out at each SAG so that the support team knew who was on the road and who had passed through. Leaving the SAG I linked up with Pete and two other riders, Robert and Emil. Robert was one of the support team and lived in Riverside, today's destination. Over the next few miles I discovered that

Robert was a great guy with a big heart and a big personality. We chatted easily as we rolled along learning about each other's riding experiences. Emil was from Switzerland and was more reserved, possibly I suspected because English was not his first language. Pete... well he's Scottish so make of that what you will! We made good progress until I was late signalling a pothole causing Pete to ride straight into it and puncture his rear tyre. Pete bore his misfortune and my poor etiquette with good grace. Following a tube change we were soon rolling again.

Passing through a succession of districts the density of business premises and housing reduced. The housing, offices and industrial units were also newer so there was an atmosphere of greater affluence. In the distance I could see some hills which were gradually getting closer. They were dissected by numerous ravines, gullies and small canyons – scenery that I had seen before but only in films and on television. We rode parallel to Route 91, sometimes passing over and under it on a fabulously smooth tarmac surface. The highway was incredibly busy with each of its six lanes full of traffic – mostly coming towards us and onward to Los Angeles.

As we entered the hills we turned onto the Santa Ana Bike trail, another wonderfully surfaced route, and gradually headed upwards to the second SAG. With the sun now shining brightly and the air gradually warming it proved to be just the spot to grab some fruit and top up my water bottles.

Resisting the temptation to linger in the sunshine we headed off again on the final leg of the stage. This proved to be the best part of the day. We rolled gradually downhill and onto another long straight avenue. Now, we were riding amongst some lovely properties with substantial houses and well-tended gardens. The avenue was lined with mature palm trees. For miles and miles, beautifully coloured rose bushes marked the central reservation. In places I spotted orange groves, heavy with their brightly coloured fruit. What a wonderful way to end a great first day! As we neared our destination Robert took on the mantle of tour guide and shared a few snippets about his home town, Riverside.

Seventy-nine miles and seven hours after setting off we arrived at our hotel for the night, another Marriott Courtyard Inn where check-in was a breeze. I took my bike to my room to find my two bags were already in there and the air conditioning had been turned on. All that was missing was a cold beer. Like the professional racing riders do, I jumped into the shower, fully clothed to wash my riding gear. Once I'd peeled off the lycra it was time to wash myself. Then after getting dressed, wringing out the lycra, rolling it in a towel and hanging it up to dry overnight I went in search of some post-stage recovery fuel, today, a milkshake and a slice of lemon drizzle cake to complete my end of ride refuelling. Within an hour of arriving, Pete and I were sitting round the hotel pool in the sunshine, enjoying a refreshing a bottle of beer and reflecting on our first stage. I had a sneaky feeling that, based on today, this tour was going to be a blast.

Stage 2: Monday 14 May, Riverside to Indio (93 Miles)

One of the most important pieces of information we were given was the cue sheet for each day's riding. This provided a mile by mile, turn by turn set of instructions with additional information on any significant route and safety points. The evening before, or on the morning of each stage, the route sheet forms the agenda for our Route Raps. Although I also have the route loaded onto my Garmin, the technology is not infallible, as regular readers will know from past events. So the route sheets provide an additional level of assurance.

Two things caught my eye on the second day's cue sheet which covered the 93 miles from Riverside to Indio. At 1.5 miles 'begin 3-mile climb' and then at 31.4 miles 'begin 6-mile climb'.

So the early part of today after leaving Riverside was going to be largely uphill. But first, let me share a morsel of Riverside's history with you. The city was founded in the early 1870s and it was here that the Californian citrus fruit industry was started in 1871 when Eliza Tibbets received three navel orange trees from Bahia in Brazil. Two of the trees survived – the other was apparently trampled by a cow! One of the two survivors was subsequently transplanted in 1903 by President Theodore Roosevelt. To cut a long story short, cuttings taken from the trees were hugely successful and some would say, led to the second Californian Gold Rush – oranges. So there you are. Now, let's get back to the ride.

I was soon onto the first hill which was fairly gentle by European standards, and as I spun my way upwards I was amused by the sight of slow-moving queues of cars with people going to work as I was going to 'play'. While waiting at one of the many traffic lights on the climb a car pulled alongside me and I heard the whir of an electric window winding down accompanied by the hiss of cold, airconditioned air escaping from within. Looking across to my left I could see the driver who was dressed in a dark suit, white shirt and tie. Then, a voice spoke asking me: "Where are you going?" "Boston" was my reply. This was met with silence and no other reaction that I could discern so, unsure as to whether or not my traffic-light neighbour had heard me, I repeated myself. "Boston. Boston, Massachusetts." There was a distinct pause and then came the reply: "Man, you're shittin' me," followed by the sound of the window winding up and the driver heading off in his airconditioned comfort. Three cheers for the long-distance cyclist!

Reaching the top of the climb, a small group of us formed up and we headed along to the first SAG stop at 23 miles on the forecourt of a gas station. After refuelling we set off for the next climb up to Beaumont. With a long ascent ahead of me I got into a lower gear and tapped out a rhythm to get to the top. In front of me in the distance I could see another rider, Cathy, who hails from San Francisco, in her distinctive white jersey. I have learnt through bitter experience to resist the temptation to up the pace and chase. I just carried on spinning at a cadence of about 90 RPM and keeping my heart rate at about 130 BPM. These are the two numbers that matter to me when climbing steady ascents like this one. Slowly but surely I could see that the gap was closing and over the next 3 to 4 miles I got to within about 300 yards of her. But that was the last I saw of her all day as, looking back over my shoulder I realised there was a spectacular view so I stopped to get a photo.

By now the temperature was rising so I pulled over at a gas station to buy a cold soda and Pete and David, who's from Maine, joined me to cool off. We then headed over to Beaumont, linked up with Emil and turned east. With a gentle downhill profile, a strong tailwind, and a good surface, we whizzed along at a cracking pace eating up the miles. This was riding at its easiest. My average speed for the first 10 miles was 15 miles per hour; my average over miles 50-60 was 25 miles per hour. For the record, my average for the whole day worked out at 17.6 miles per hour.

We rode along beside, and sometimes on, the interstate (I-10) which was a totally new experience for me since apart from a couple of closed road events I have never ridden on a motorway. Apparently the low density of roads in this part of California means that cycling on the interstate was legal. Although we were riding at a fabulous speed I could feel the temperature rising and it eventually peaked at 34°C (93°F) and I was glad of the breeze in my face as I cut through the air. Approaching Palm Springs we passed by a massive series of wind farms. Compared to the wind farms in the North Sea, which I am familiar with from my coastal rides back home, these farms were huge, both in terms of the area they covered and also the height of the individual turbines. There are over 3,000 individual turbines on the site, which are between 80 and 160 feet high. Most were turning gracefully in the wind. I wondered what the electricity output they generated was.

Our route took us round the edge of Palm Springs. Since the early 1900s this has been a resort city – initially for health seekers benefitting from the dry climate and subsequently for more sporting and artistic pursuits. Palm Springs is also the place where the 'Desert Modern' style of high-end architecture originated – open-designs, wall to wall carpeting, air-conditioning, big plate glass windows and not forgetting the swimming pools. As we passed the city I was reminded of an oasis in the desert, which of course it is!

Leaving Palm Springs at around 2:30pm we turned onto a long boulevard heading east which was accompanied by the thud, thud, thud of a flat tyre. Puncture! Pete was the unlucky rider. In the baking heat and with little shelter it was a challenge to remove his rear wheel, lever off the tyre and replace the tube. The culprit seemed to be a small thorn. Pete's 2:30pm, puncture became a regular feature of our riding over the next few days. So regular that I could almost set my watch by it.

From Palm Springs we continued on the final 10-mile leg to our destination at Indio. As we rode along I was struck by the large billboards lining the roadside advertising seemingly every consumer product or service imaginable. I even spotted one with the face of the Permatan President himself. He seemed to be hustling some sort of property deal – there's a surprise. Talking of billboards, indulge me as I make a small diversion in today's story. If you haven't seen the film *Three Billboards Outside Ebbing, Missouri* then you simply must. Frances McDormand who plays the lead alongside Woody Harrelson, won a richly deserved Best Actress Oscar. I watched it shortly before I left the UK. Her acceptance speech set a new benchmark. Now, whenever I saw a billboard I automatically think of Frances and the wonderful, yet tragic, story she tells.

With the temperature reaching the afternoon peak and the possibility that my Gatorade drink was approaching boiling point I was glad to make the final turn into our hotel in Indio for the evening. This was a fast day. This was a hot day. But most of all this was a thoroughly enjoyable day.

One of the features of extended tours like this is that time is very precious. Unless our hotel is right in the middle of town I don't usually get a chance to look around and explore. All I can tell you is that Indio sits on the edge of the desert and has a casino. How do I know this? Well, I had dinner in the casino!

It was quite an eye-opener to me as I strolled past the rows and rows of slot machines and various gaming tables. I have little interest in gambling. My only experience of it was many years ago when a friend took me to a casino in Leeds. After exchanging £10 for some chips I sat down at one of the roulette tables and placed my chips down. The croupier, who I vaguely remember was very alluring, spun the wheel and eventually the ball came to rest. It was quite hypnotic watching it roll around the wheel. Then the croupier used a sort of rake to gather up the chips and it dawned on me that I had lost! Realising that for me at least, this was a mugs game I have stayed away from the gaming tables ever since. Of course, like many others I have had a flutter or three on the lottery or taken part in the office Grand National sweepstake.

The other thing that struck me was the food on offer. A help yourself carvery style buffet with massive piles of different roast meats, fish dishes, pies, vegetables and so forth. There was also a wide range of sweet, sticky deserts. As far as I could work out, you paid your money and then ate as much as you wanted. There were a lot of people there eating a lot of food. My portions, which

I thought were large and reflected a hard day in the saddle, were miniscule in comparison to those of some of the other diners that I saw. For many of them repeat visits to reload seemed to be the order of the day.

Stage 3: Tuesday 15 May, Indio to Blythe (97 Miles)

Day 3, a ride of 97 miles from Indio to Blythe, saw a number of firsts for me at least. The major feature of the day was that it was the first full stage in the desert. And we rode it on the interstate (I-10). Imagine, UK readers, riding along the hard shoulder of the M1 for about 80 miles! The only difference was that there was much less traffic. With temperatures in the mid-thirties centigrade (mid-nineties, fahrenheit), keeping cool and staying hydrated were the keys to surviving. For the first time in my cycling life I wore a pair of Factor 50 arm coolers to protect my arms from the sun. In the UK if I cover my arms with anything other than a long sleeve jersey I wear arm warmers – to keep warm! On the hydration front, in addition to the two water bottles that I normally carry I was also wearing a Camelbak with an extra 2 litres of water. This was a Christmas present from my daughter, Megan. I also made sure that I had a copious supply of Factor 30 sun cream to slap on and protect my skin from burning. At this juncture, readers, I would just like to report that my tan lines were progressing nicely and the pasty white skin that earlier I feared might be the source of some merriment for the other riders, was rapidly disappearing.

My goodness, will you look at that. Yet again I seem to have drifted off the subject with another little diversion. Let's get back to the main event. After leaving Indio we crossed over the San Andreas fault line. I'm not exactly sure where we passed over it as the earth certainly didn't move for me. Then it was on to the only climb of the day a nice long, steady 12-mile ascent. This wasn't especially steep and once again it was a case of getting in the right gear and tapping out a steady rhythm. From time to time I got out of the saddle to stretch my back and as I often do, indulge in a little dance on the pedals – a brisk foxtrot today, if you really want to know. There's almost nothing better than a good bike ride with a spot of dancing along the way!

The main challenge today was the heat as I was riding directly into the sun and I was sweating quite profusely. Every 10 minutes or so I took a couple of swigs of water from my Camelbak to stay hydrated. It took me around one hour to reach the summit where the landscape opened out dramatically. Although we were still climbing gently, on what was almost a false flat, I could see the desert stretching for miles ahead and on either side. We were riding along a broad valley, several miles wide and flanked on either side by rock bluffs. The vast scale of the landscape here was quite overwhelming.

Ahead, the road stretched as far as the eye could see. As we rode along, I really did feel quite insignificant in such a big landscape. A glance at the map told me that we were riding along the southern edge of the Joshua Tree National Park – celebrated in the eponymous album of the same name by Irish rockers U2. A road sign caught my eye – if I left the interstate I could either go north into the Park or south to Mecca. Unusual place names intrigue me so I made a mental note to do some post-stage research on the Interweb.

Readers, I can now reveal that Mecca, which is a small farming community, does indeed derive its name from the other, rather more famous place. It's quite an interesting story too. Spanish missionaries brought some date palm trees with them and found the area ideal for their growth. Subsequently, a group of farm workers from the area travelled to the Middle East to learn more about growing dates and source other varieties. On their return, one of the group, a lady called Flora Belote, decided to name their Californian community after the Arabian city. Now the region grows palms bearing the most prized of all dates, the Medjool variety which is a personal favourite of mine. If you've never tried one you simply must. Their sweet caramelised, honeyed flavour and their succulent texture will leave you drooling. Nowadays, Mecca hosts an annual Date Festival every February. I've made a note to return someday. Rumour has it that there are dates the size of apples to be had.

Leaving Mecca behind me for another day I carried straight on eventually reaching the first SAG where I gladly, no gleefully, refilled my water containers. I had already drunk nearly two litres and we were still in the 'cool' part of the day. Alongside the rest area was a tank museum dedicated to General George Patton of World War II fame. (He was born in California.)

We (Pete, David, Emil and me) headed back onto the interstate and with a tail wind and a gentle downhill profile organised ourselves with a spot of through and off, each taking it in turns to lead for about a mile before peeling off and tucking in at the back of the line. Riding at around 25 miles per hour meant that we had to keep a careful lookout for debris, mainly the remains of truck tyres that had blown out, which if hit could cause serious damage. The real challenge, though, was that the blowouts left small needle-sized metal fragments which embedded themselves in our tyres leading to punctures. Pete, Emil and I each had a rear wheel puncture as a consequence. And let me tell you, replacing a tube in the middle of the desert in the middle of the day with no shelter for miles is not a lot of fun! I was in luck as I discovered my puncture at the final SAG of the day so at least I had the benefit of both some shade and a track pump with a pressure gauge to inflate the new tube.

Riding along the interstate wasn't anything like as bad as I had feared. Most of the truck drivers pulled over to the outside lane when it was clear, giving us an extra berth. Quite a few gave us a friendly toot on their horns. I suspect that they must have thought we were quite mad when they passed us. There was one stretch which was very rough due to frost cracks so we christened it 'The California Cobbles' and imagined that we were riding Paris-Roubaix. There's an irony for me here since CV was originally designed by Bianchi specifically for the Paris-Roubaix, otherwise known as The Hell of The North. It is one of the toughest one-day races on the European professional racing calendar. First held in 1896, the race takes place over numerous bike and body breaking cobbled 'roads'. It is a true test of bike handling skills, fitness, stamina and sheer determination. I can report that CV surpassed herself on the California Cobbles. I think I did quite well too.

The long-distance views and the straights were incredible. I will no longer complain about boredom again when riding in the Fens back at home. Compared to the interstate, the Fenland roads are nothing. As we rode along I could feel the temperature rising to its peak at around 35°C (95°F). I was getting through my water at a fast rate – both drinking it and also spraying it on my head and arm coolers. At our final SAG we were able to get some stockings packed with ice to wrap around our necks as an additional coolant. And very cool they were too!

Eventually we left the interstate after riding on it for nearly 90 miles! By now, the combination of copious amounts of sun screen and desert dust on my skin meant that I looked like a tramp. But I felt pretty good. Tired and worn out, yes. But exhilarated too. I had survived the desert! The ride had one final delight in store for me. As we approached Blythe, Pete commented that the view of the road stretching for several miles ahead would make an iconic photograph. I pulled over to get the camera out while Pete carried on shouting over his shoulder that I would soon catch up with him. Iconic photo snapped, I got back on CV only to discover that I had a front wheel puncture (another of those metal fragments). What bad luck, just a few miles from the finish. As I was pumping up the tyre another rider, Ichiro, who comes from San Francisco and who I haven't seen much of so far, caught up with me. So we rode in together and had a nice little chat.

After having my usual clothing and body shower and the route rap for tomorrow we all gathered together for dinner, a catered barbeque. With the help of a can of cold beer, the efforts of the day were soon behind me and I was enjoying that warm glow that riders who have had a long and demanding day in the saddle will recognise. And guess what... we're going to do it all again tomorrow. Yay!

Stage 4: Wednesday 16 May, Blythe to Wickenburg (116 Miles)

Today started where yesterday ended. Well obviously it did! I stepped out of the same hotel which I had arrived at yesterday evening. We were back on the interstate (I-10) for another stint of riding alongside the trucks while dodging the potentially tyre shredding debris that lies on the hard shoulder. Once again, most truckers moved to the outside lane to avoid battering us with their tail draughts. For some reason, Americans refer to the outside lane as the inside lane. For the avoidance of doubt therefore when I say outside lane I mean the one nearest the middle of the highway. So there!

I can remember doing time trials in the 1970s on the Great North Road, the A1 in Lincolnshire and Nottinghamshire. Then it was deemed a good tactic to ride as close to the carriageway as you dared in order to benefit from the suction effect of the air as the trucks passed by. Over a 25-mile time trial it was reckoned that you could gain a few precious seconds. Today, though, I kept my distance!

We reached a significant point today after only 5 miles and left California, the Golden State, and crossed into Arizona, the Grand Canyon State. Only another 13 States to go... I was beginning to get a sense of the scale of this nation. Covering around 164 million square miles, California is the third largest state in the country. By comparison the UK covers about 94 million square miles. California has a population of 40 million; the figure for the UK is 67 million. That means each Californian 'has' just over 4 square miles of territory and each UK citizen 'has' around 1.5 square miles. What does all this mean? Probably that the UK is a more crowded place than California. Can't say that I really noticed!

After pausing to record our first state crossing, we started our exploration of Arizona with a 7-mile climb. In fact most of today's stage was uphill, gently uphill. As I climbed steadily upwards I could feel the sun doing its work and the air temperature was steadily rising. According to my Garmin it peaked at around 35°C (95°F). This was going to be one long hot day. At 22 miles we swung off the interstate and into a service station to nab a cold drink and top up our water bottles as we still had over 20 miles to reach the first SAG. The local Burger King was on hand to provide our fare. I snagged what I thought was a banana milkshake from the fridge but after opening it I realised that I was actually holding a small bottle of skimmed milk! Oh well, it's all protein.

Heading out of the service area and back onto the interstate we could see the road stretching ahead of us for miles and miles. This was to be the defining feature of today's ride – long, straight roads. After a couple of miles, the route notes announced 'Begin 10-mile climb' so it was back into a low gear to spin along. To be sure I'm not misleading you, the climbs here are very gradual and rarely above three or four per cent. Most of the time they rise at around 1 per cent with an occasional kick upwards. Ahead of us as we moved along I spotted a couple of riders on touring bikes complete with front and rear panniers. As we drew alongside we slowed for a brief chat – one of the benefits of riding on such a wide shoulder. It transpired that one of the pair had set off from Halifax, Nova Scotia earlier this year and had already traversed the USA and was now heading for Argentina. Yes, you read that right – Argentina! As I wished him well and bade him farewell I have to say that I felt rather feeble. My own attempt to cross the US of A seemed rather trivial by comparison. As I reflected on what such a huge tour would entail I started dreaming of riding what might be the ultimate end to end ride: Alaska to Argentina (Tiera del Fuego). Well, I'd better get to Boston first.

After about 36 miles we finally said goodbye to I-10. And yes, I did say goodbye, and good riddance. Well, actually I shouted "Goodbye and Good Riddance". I can't say that I especially enjoyed the experience of riding the interstate but I did appreciate the pragmatism as it was the only way to travel east hereabouts without adding significantly to our total mileage. Swinging on to US Route 60 was a delight. It was mostly a well surfaced road though one stretch was pretty rough with tar filled frost cracks. As there was virtually no traffic I was able to spend more time looking at the surrounding landscape. By the time we reached the first SAG in the hamlet of Brenda at 44 miles I was frying. The sun was beating down and the desert landscape stretched for miles in every direction. Diving into the gas station I emerged with a Double Caramel Magnum ice cream. Quite simply the perfect coolant on what was now an exceptionally hot day. As we still had over 70 miles to go, we watered up, signed out and headed back down the road.

As I was riding along I tried to describe the landscape to myself. I'm going to try and share this with you. It was a landscape that I have seen a thousand times before, but only on television or in the cinema. Close up there was sand, lots of sand which was covered in small scrubby bushes. As we headed east I noticed that the proportion of cactus trees was gradually increasing – the classic multi limbed type that appear in almost every cowboy film. The land was largely devoid of visible animal life, just the occasional lizard scurrying for cover and a few birds of prey circling lazily above us like vultures waiting to swoop should we fall. Maybe they were vultures? The air was remarkably clear so visibility was excellent. In the far distance and on either side were a series of bluffs and low hills with higher mountains even further away. In the distance we saw a couple of dust devils – sand bearing whirlwinds. Fortunately they were moving away from us.

It was incredibly hard to judge distances. At one stage I could see the road stretching out in front of me in a straight line and I picked out a point which I guessed was about 5 miles away. After riding at an average speed of 18 miles per hour for 20 minutes I seemed to be no nearer. In fact it took me about 50 minutes to reach the point I had selected. The scale of the landscape here was simply breathtaking. Riding through it on a bicycle brought home the enormity of the country. Later on, when looking at a wall map of Arizona and the route we had traversed, it was pretty sobering to discover that we had only made a minor scratch on the side of the state. Humbling is probably the best word to describe my feelings. I feel quite incapable of accurately describing what I experienced today. All I can say is come and see it for yourselves. And at the risk of piling superlative upon superlative, what I saw today was but one small part of this enormous country. There is more to see – much, much more as I hoped to discover in the days ahead.

Staying hydrated out here was a major consideration. Even with two water bottles and my Camelbak the rate I was drinking my water meant that I had to be very aware of opportunities to refill. Failure to pay attention to my hydration needs risked the onset of heat exhaustion, or worse. Back home in the UK I usually don't need to drink very much and my metabolism has adapted to this. One 600 millilitre bottle with a couple of stops to buy a drink, coffee or a soda, can keep me going for at least 100 miles, even in the summer. Anticipating a rather different scenario on this tour I had experimented with different approaches on my training rides in the UK. What worked best for me was taking a small sip about every 10 minutes. So that's what I did and when I remembered, which wasn't very often, I programmed my Garmin to beep every 10 minutes as a reminder.

In the heat of the early afternoon I was finding the riding quite tough, both physically and mentally. According to the route notes there was a gas station a few miles up the road at the appropriately named settlement of Hope. It's too small to be thought of as a town or even a village. So hope kept me going and I kept going to Hope, eking out my water to ensure I didn't run out before I arrived. Eventually I could see the gas station ahead of me with a few other riders milling around the forecourt. As I arrived I realised that the gas station was shut and looked like it had been shut for quite some time – days or even weeks. Not just for the afternoon. Like me, my fellow riders had been counting on the gas station as a source of fresh water. And like me, their reserves were minimal. We spent a bit of time chatting to each other trying to work out our options. There was no mobile phone reception so we were unable ask the tour organisers to come back with water for us. In fact we were a bit surprised that, as they must have passed by the gas station before us, they hadn't organised an impromptu water stop given that it was several miles to the next SAG.

Well, fortunately we got lucky in the most unexpected and surreal way. A scene unfolded that any Hollywood director, Lucas, Spielberg or Tarantino would have been proud of. Imagine a swirling, heraldic soundtrack by John Williams or Max Richter.

I'm giving this a big build up readers. Quite deliberately, for this was one of those moments on the tour that I will never forget. As the music swelled and grew George, Stephen or Quentin shouted "Action" and a massive RV, a recreational vehicle, glided silently onto the forecourt from behind the gas station. I don't think I have ever seen a bigger RV. It stopped and the engine was switched off. As if to torture me, I could hear the hissing and ticking of air conditioning oozing from within the vehicle.

Then, the driver's door opened and a man in his mid-forties emerged followed by his wife. They strolled over to us and said "Hi". We chatted with them and then asked if they had any water that they could spare. Without a second glance they turned and climbed back into the RV. Unsure as to whether or not our cry for help had been favourably received we stood around looking at each other. After a short pause, the couple emerged again. Their outstretched arms were laden with boxes containing bottles of mineral water. They laid them down on the tarmac by the petrol pumps and in the shade of the forecourt, telling us to help ourselves as there was plenty more where they came from.

We all fell on the water like locusts descending on a choice crop. After slaking our thirsts we refilled our water bottles and Camelbaks. Our saviours replenished the stocks from within their RV. They even apologised for being short of ice! We thanked them profusely and tried to pay for their water. The wife refused point bank to accept any money, telling us that they would receive sufficient reward in heaven!

Repeating our thanks and saying our goodbyes we headed off back into the desert on the final leg of the day's stage. As I left, I noticed a billboard at the side of the road. It read 'You Are Now Beyond Hope'. I reflected on how true that could have been. Like many other riders I was so roasted that this could have been game over. The end of my EFI. A faint alarm bell was ringing at the back of my overheated brain regarding the tour logistics and rider support. I tucked it away, for now. But with the kindness of strangers I was still alive and on the road.

Most of the rest of the day continued in this vein. Hot, hot temperatures and long, long roads. With 9 miles to go, relief came in the form of a nice fast downhill run into Wickenburg, our overnight base. Although I was hot and frazzled, I had my shower, washed my kit and headed to a local saloon bar for dinner. I felt pretty good and looked back on a hard, challenging day's riding but a day that had brought unexpected rewards. Today was the longest day of the tour. I had completed my first ever century ride, 116 miles, in the USA. That was an achievement in itself.

Stage 5: Thursday 17 May, Wickenburg to Prescott (60 Miles)

Thus far the tour has been pretty flat. And by that I mean flat in terms of the terrain, not in terms of interest. Well, today that all changed. The GPS track promised nearly 60 miles with just over 6,000 feet of climbing and a maximum gradient of 16 per cent. The route profile showed two climbs, at 20 miles and again at 35 miles. The route notes also mentioned a succession of false flats and false summits along the way. After the largely flat and straight roads of the past few days I was looking forward to some climbing. I do like a good climb!

The four of us, David, Emil, Pete and I rolled out of Wickenburg along a beautifully smooth highway – described as a scenic route. Another hot day under cloudless blue skies beckoned. Even the wind seemed to be co-operating. In the far distance I could see the range of hills that we were heading towards. Judging from the roadside billboards and signs that we passed this was very definitely Republican territory. I passed a large billboard which protested against Hillary Clinton in the most direct way imaginable. In order to spare your blushes readers, and a desire not to lay myself open to a charge of libel I won't repeat what I saw! And just a few miles further up the road was a large sign imploring the Permatan President to take the USA out of NATO.

On the stages we had already ridden I had been impressed by the consideration of the motorists, car drivers and truckers that we were sharing the tarmac with. Most gave us a wide berth when overtaking and often a friendly toot on the horn as they passed us by. Even when they have had to slow because of oncoming traffic the majority were very patient, waiting their moment to pass safely. A very small minority were pushy, blasting their horns and overtaking a hairs breadth away from us. Unfortunately, today we experienced a spot of road rage when one driver passed me, blasting his horn and then slowed down and shouted "Get the [expletive] off the road". As regular readers will know, my usual response to aggressive drivers is to wave at them like they are my new best friends as they pass me by. As long as my physical safety isn't threatened, life is just too short to get overly wound up. Today, I decided that no response was the best response. By all accounts, I got off lightly, with only a spot of verbal abuse and a mile or so up the road ahead of me, Emil was virtually run off the road by the same driver and was pretty shaken up by the experience. A phone call was made to the Highway Patrol to report the incident. I don't know whether or not they eventually caught up with the driver. They did promise to step up their patrols on the road but I never saw any of their distinctive black and white vehicles.

After sharing a few perspectives on the incident while we refreshed ourselves in the shade of a gas station forecourt, we set off again to begin the first climb of the day, a 7-mile ascent to Yarnell Pass. With a long straight approach I could see the challenge that lay ahead. As I was tapping out my rhythm in the pedals a sign caught my eye – a turning to Stanton. This confused me momentarily as I thought I was back in my home village of Stanton in Suffolk! The town was originally a stagecoach stop called Antelope Halt. A few years after gold was found in the area in 1863, a businessman, Chuck Stanton moved in and with the help of some Mexican bandits, literally took over the town. Having disposed of any opposition, Stanton ruled the roost for some years until he was eventually killed by a Mexican gunman. The town continued to enjoy a colourful reputation for many years thereafter. By the late 1960s it was virtually uninhabited and was eventually redeveloped as an RV park with some of the old buildings including the saloon, dance hall, town jail and Chuck Stanton's house being restored. Now the RV park is open for around six months each year. 'My' Stanton can trace its origins back to Roman times but has a much less colourful history.

Gradually the road ascended and I could see it rising up the hillside ahead of me. Gaining height through a series of hairpins I was reminded of some of the climbs of the Pyrenees. Long and gradual with spectacular views back downhill. I stopped to take lots of photos. My Strava stats show that the segment was 8 miles, rose 1,900 feet to 4,850 feet with an average gradient of 4 per cent. I completed it in 54 minutes. Not especially quick, but then I did stop to take those pictures.

Cresting the summit at Yarnell I arrived at the day's first SAG to find the cheery faces of the support team, Mary and Robin, cheering us in. This was a welcome halt as I had been drinking copious amounts of water and needed to refill my bottles. Yarnell achieved tragic notoriety in 2013 when 19 firefighters, the Granite Mountain Hotshots, were killed while fighting a bushfire started by lightening. The fire devastated over 8,000 acres of land in the area. The tragedy has been captured in the film *Only the Brave*, released in 2017, with a cast including Miles Teller, Josh Brolin, Jeff Bridges and Jennifer Connolly.

As we descended, the character of the countryside changed dramatically. Gone was the arid scrub of the desert, replaced for a few miles at least by a more pastoral, farmed landscape with horses grazing under shady groves of trees. I noticed that several of the properties had signs for Maughan Ranches which I subsequently discovered extends over 500,000 acres of land in Arizona divided across 15 individual ranching units. That is one big operation! After returning to the desert landscape for a while we passed through the graphically named Skull Valley to reach a store located in what literally felt like the middle of nowhere. With the final climb ahead of us this was the ideal time to recharge our batteries with cold drinks and ice creams. Despite being in a fairly isolated location there was a steady trickle of local people calling in to get their essential supplies. The proprietor looked as if she had won the lottery serving the hungry and thirsty cyclists. I'm guessing that her turnover for the month of May showed a substantial upturn. So yes, cycling is good for the local economy.

Resisting the temptation to linger we set off on the final climb of the day, 11.7 miles ascending over 1,000 feet at an average of 2 per cent. This was quite a different climb to the one to Yarnell. Much gentler with many more curves and hairpins broken up by some false summits. The other main difference was that we were now amongst a forest of ponderosa pines. In the heat of the afternoon sun, the air was filled with the scent of pine oil. And talking about the air, the higher we got the clearer and cleaner it seemed. Quite a contrast from that of smog laden Los Angeles at the start of the week. This was a climb that I really enjoyed and almost didn't want to end. But all good things must come to an end so cresting the final ridge I was greeted by the magnificent sight of a fast, smooth road snaking its way downhill.

I put CV into her highest gear and we wound it up and let rip. CV responded magnificently to the challenge and led me downhill and effortlessly through a succession of sweeping curves. I could see from my Garmin that the mileage to the stage end was rapidly falling. All to soon I was into Prescott and at my hotel. And let me share a little secret with you. Arriving at the hotel I discovered that I had joined the Mile-High Club. No, not that one – tut, tut for thinking such thoughts readers! Founded in 1864 and lying at an altitude of 5,400 feet Prescott markets itself as Arizona's Mile High City! On that note I headed out to see what delights the city had to offer the weary cyclist.

There's a little footnote, literally, to today's stage report. With the heat of the day my feet had been swelling rather more than I'm used to. Consequently, by early to mid-afternoon my riding shoes, particularly the left one, had become quite cramped. Harnessing the power of the Interweb I did a spot of giggling and discovered that just up the road from the hotel was the High Gear Bicycle Shop. Co-owner Cindy Alward, a delightful person, was on hand to fit me up with a new larger pair of shoes. She was even happy to measure and fit my cleats. The shop was a great place to visit and has an interesting display of old, steel-framed bikes. If you happen to be passing by I recommend that you drop in. And on that foot(note) dinner beckoned…

Stage 6: Friday 18 May, Prescott to Cottonwood (46 Miles)

At only 46 miles long, the sixth stage from Prescott to Cottonwood was a comparatively short day so there was the possibility of fitting in some sightseeing en route. Of course, the whole ride was really one massive sightseeing experience but today I hoped I might be able to get out of the saddle and walk around like a tourist! Waking up I could see that another sunny, cloudless day lay ahead. After a breakfast of fruit, yoghurt, scrambled eggs on toast, croissant and coffee I was ready to roll down the road by 7:30am.

The first part of the ride out of Prescott was very straightforward and although the roads were busy with people going to work it wasn't too unpleasant. Unfortunately that soon changed when we turned on to Highway 89 where the traffic was pretty intense. It was a vivid reminder of recent days on the California interstate but today the road actually seemed busier if that were possible. Fortunately, we only had to ride about seven miles before turning on to State Route 89A and the start of the day's main event – the ascent of Mingus Mountain. Mingus Mountain – that has a certain ring to it, doesn't it?

Ahead of me I could see the road stretching towards the ridge of mountains several miles away. Looking just beyond my front wheel the gradient was barely discernible but looking ahead I could tell that the road rose gradually upwards – climbing about 1,300 feet over the next 10 miles. This was a classic false flat. Once again the scale of the landscape here was simply immense and I could see for several miles in every direction. Looking at the elevation reading on my Garmin I was surprised to see that I was already over 5,000 feet above sea level. Unfamiliar heights indeed for Captain Century who was more used to riding below sea level in the Fens of East Anglia. The air around me was incredibly clear and pure – very refreshing. Above me I watched what I think was an eagle (it had a huge wingspan) lazily circling around looking for its next meal. This was one of those special occasions where I felt totally at one with CV and my surroundings. Man, machine and nature. Bliss! CV purred along nicely too so I guess she was also pretty content.

Gradually the natural ponderosa pine forest got closer and with a gentle turn I was on to the mountain proper. With a light press on my gear shifter I dropped onto the small chain ring, moved down the cassette a couple of cogs and started spinning at a cadence (80-85 RPM) that I hoped I could sustain to the top of the climb about 10 miles and 2,000 feet ahead.

With an amazingly smooth surface, the road meandered its way up the mountain mostly through gentle curves with a few classic hairpins which brought back happy memories of riding in the Pyrenees a couple of years ago. Interestingly, the gradient on the hairpins tended to be steeper than in Europe where on many climbs the gradient eases off on the hairpins. With relatively few cars on the road I was often able to pick a line towards the centre of the road on right hand curves and cheat the gradient. On left hand curves I stuck to the high side and eased down as I exited thereby both maintaining my cadence and speed. From time to time I slipped up into a higher gear and got out of the saddle to stretch my back and give my legs a little action. Then, easing back into a lower gear I settled back into my rhythm and enjoyed tapping out the miles. I always look forward to opportunities to dance in my pedals. Given the length of the climb, today was definitely a day for a waltz and not the tango!

I stopped a couple of times to admire and photograph the views where several hundred feet below me I could see road I had already ridden dotted with other riders also making their way upwards. With relatively little traffic much of the ascent was fairly quiet so I was able to enjoy the sights and smells that I passed through. With the morning sun warming the pines there was a lovely delicate scent in the air which was really invigorating. As I approached the top of the climb I just felt so lucky to be able to enjoy an experience like this.

Cresting the summit of Mingus Mountain (7,023 feet) I saw the smiling faces of Mary and Robin which meant that I had arrived at the SAG. Pulling in, my enjoyment was made all the more complete when I spotted a rider with a celeste Bianchi Sempre who had just ridden up from the other side with a friend.

Then, after snacking on some fruit and posing for the obligatory summit photo I set off on the descent with David, Emil and Pete. We seem to have established ourselves as a quartet. Now readers, if you thought that my description of the ascent was engaging I have to say that I am struggling to find the words to describe the descent.

From a riding perspective it was everything the ascent was – smooth surfaces, long straights, sweeping curves with the occasional hairpins which meant that I could sit back in the saddle and let CV do her work. She was the star of the show; I was just a supporting actor. Picking a line into the corners, leaning hard over and letting CV pull us through the curves was exhilarating. All I needed to do was give the brakes an occasional touch to scrub off some speed quickly and reassuringly just before the entering each bend.

All of a sudden we burst out of the trees and below I could see the most magnificent views with the road snaking its way downwards. As this wasn't enough ahead of me at the bottom of the mountain, the landscape stretched away for at least 30 miles with red tinged mountains acting as a sort of frame or reference point for the vista. This is where we will be heading tomorrow and I can't wait!

As today was a short day we had decided to stop in Jerome, an historic mining town, for lunch. David, who had been here a couple of weeks before recommended a place to eat. This was a chance to have my first proper American hamburger and I wasn't disappointed. I chose the Arizona Special with a side salad and it was delicious. With only a few miles to go to our destination the four of us, together with Eve, Emil's wife, enjoyed a leisurely lunch. And big thanks to Emil for treating us. I also took the opportunity to visit Caduceus Cellars to buy a t-shirt for my son Huw. The rock group Tool is a favourite of Huw's and their lead singer, Maynard James Keenan, a US Army veteran is the winemaker and owner of Caduceus Cellars and Merkin Vineyards. Over the last 10 years, when he's not rocking and rolling, Keenan has been a driving force in the development of Arizona's wine industry

After lunch we rode a couple of miles further downhill and detoured slightly off the route to visit the Jerome Historic State Park. This commemorates the town's copper mining heritage and we had a look around the visitor centre which has an interesting collection of mining artefacts and photographs as well as a fascinating film telling the story of Jerome. The mining industry took off in the early 1880s when William A. Clarke bought out the existing mining interests, constructed a narrow-gauge railway link to the main network and developed the operation to new levels of production. The Audrey Shaft, completed in 1918, descends some 1,900 feet. With the water table sitting at 1,300 feet, pumping water out of the mine was a major consideration. Mining operations continued here until 1953. Since that time Jerome has reinvented itself as a popular tourist destination and achieved National Historic Landscape Status in 1967. The throngs of people in the large assortment of gift shops show that this has been entirely successful.

After a good look around we continued down the descent for a further five miles arriving at our overnight destination, Cottonwood, unusually early at 2:30pm. We all agreed that today we had enjoyed an excellent day at the 'office' with a good working lunch! And the new shoes which I bought yesterday seemed to have done the job – no sore and swollen feet!

Stage 7: Saturday 19 May, Cottonwood to Flagstaff (47 Miles)

As I walked down the stairs from the balcony outside my room at about 6am hotel there was a real buzz in the air. The general consensus from those in the know was that today was going to be nothing short of spectacular – scenery and riding. So that set me up for the day. I couldn't wait to get started even though I found it hard to imagine how yesterday's route could be bettered. Today's route took us out of Cottonwood to Sedona and then on to Flagstaff. At 47 miles it was going to be another relatively short day in the saddle, mileagewise. From my pre-tour reading and my notes I could see that we would be riding through the Red Hills of Sedona but I didn't know any more than that.

After the route rap we rolled out of Cottonwood heading north east. Behind us I could just make out Jerome on the side of the mountain we had ridden down yesterday and above it a stretch of that thrilling descent. The first part of today's ride wasn't particularly rewarding as the road was very busy and we were being passed by a constant stream of cars and trucks. Once again the road rolled along as it rose steadily upwards. Gradually it dawned on me that the character of the landscape was changing. Gone were the browns and tans of the desert landscape which were now replaced with more greenery and a red hue to the soil. In the distance I could see some cliffs that had the same distinctive red hue. We were entering sandstone country.

Rounding a bend I was confronted by a spectacular cliff formation, weathered into towering columns and pillars. The layered, rust coloured rock faces were stunning. As we rode on, the rocks took on even more spectacular shapes and colours. I spent so much time looking around and being captivated by the views that I found it difficult to stay focussed on the road I was riding over. Arriving at Sedona we stopped for coffee at a café that had been highlighted at the route rap. The view from the terrace was quite simply amazing. I was looking at millions of years of geological history which had been shaped into the most amazing patterns and shapes. The views were almost beyond description and my photographs didn't do them justice. I could have sat here all day in the warm sunshine and soaked up the landscape. But I had to press on.

Leaving Sedona we entered a canyon which gradually closed in as we rode along it for next 12 miles. Covered with ponderosa pine, oak, ash and other deciduous tree species we were now in the part of Coconino National Forest managed by the US Forest Service. My forester's eyes took a close interest in the landscape I was riding through. At an information point along the way I discovered that the management plan for the forest had recently been updated. This piqued my professional interest so I made a note to have a look at it after the tour when I was back at home in the UK. There were lots of small attractive campsites all along the valley and as this was the weekend they all seemed busy. As we rode deeper into the valley the landscape reminded me of a Scottish Glen but on a much larger scale.

Gradually, as we reached the head of the canyon, the road began to kick up until rounding a corner I looked upwards to see it way above me. It was game on. I had arrived at the start of the climb proper. Over the next two miles the road climbed steadily upwards through a series of spectacular hairpins. As I climbed in the hot afternoon sun I could feel my breathing getting slightly more laboured – the effects of altitude. The most challenging parts of the climb were riding round the hairpins where the gradient increased noticeably before flattening off when the road straightened out again. Climbing the face of the mountain was a bit like ascending a ladder a rung at a time. As I ascended, I could see the road I had travelled below me – and it was a really satisfying feeling to be able to measure my progress.

Eventually with a final left curve I arrived at the summit at 6,400 feet and the next SAG. I rolled into the large car park and did a couple of laps spinning a low gear to relax my legs before climbing off CV. After a cold drink and some tasty strawberries, I rode over to the nearby viewpoint look down at the climb I had just completed. It was a really satisfying feeling to look down through the hairpins and back towards Sedona, several miles behind me.

On the path to the viewpoint I passed a row of stalls with Native Americans selling a selection of goods – jewellery, artwork, clothing and so forth. The surrounding area has been inhabited since 10,000 BC by Paleo-Indians who hunted game in the area. Over time, the population of hunter-gatherer tribes flourished and there is a range of rock art visible near Sedona. More recently the Yavapi and some nomadic Apache tribes settled in the area until, in 1876, they were forcibly removed. Prior to coming on the tour I read a book about American history. The chronicle started in 1492 when Columbus arrived on the east coast. I was fascinated to learn more about the history of this nation prior to 1492 but there does not seem to be much available to read. I have since learned that, unlike Europe where there are lots of written accounts, much of Native American history was never written down and instead has been passed through the generations by word of mouth. I decided to do some research when I was back home as the few glimpses I have had made it sound really fascinating.

The final leg of the day's riding took us into Flagstaff along a newly resurfaced road with the smell of fresh tarmac in the air. This was another short day and we arrived at the hotel at 2pm before our rooms were ready. So there was a chance to enjoy a cold beer and chat amongst ourselves. A bike service station had been set up in the hotel car park and I was able to wash CV, degrease her chain and give her the once over. She appreciated the spa treatment and was holding up to the rigours of the tour remarkably well. I have been really enjoying riding her and we are getting to know each other's idiosyncrasies. By way of an update I can also report that my new shoes have solved the tight foot issue – I am quite comfortable now.

We were in Flagstaff for two nights as the day after our arrival was a rest day. Pete and I used it to visit the nearby Grand Canyon which is somewhere I have always wanted to see. Before leaving the UK, I had thought it would be possible to ride there and back on the rest day. Pete was much more sensible and arranged a guided tour for us which started and finished in Flagstaff.

Having two nights in the same hotel gave me the opportunity to completely unpack my two kitbags. You would be surprised at some of the things I found lurking in there. I know I was! Hopefully, I could repack everything in a more orderly way and avoid what had now become a morning battle for supremacy – cyclist versus kitbags. So far I had come out on top; just. I was ever fearful that one morning I would succeed in breaking one of the zips, if indeed that were success.

FLAGSTAFF TO SANTA FE : 5 DAYS, 399 MILES

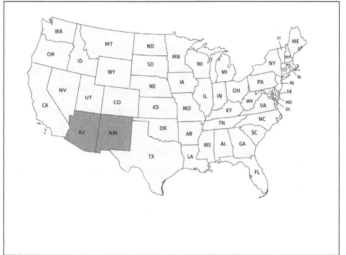

3. GETTING MY KICKS RIDING RABBITS AND STANDING ON CORNERS

Stage 8: Monday 21 May, Flagstaff to Holbrook (93 Miles)

Our visit to the Grand Canyon was superb. Pete had tracked down a small tour company, Adventure Southwest, that provided a more personal approach so at 8am we walked the mile to their depot and boarded a small minibus. Bob, our guide for the day was a walking, talking encyclopaedia of information. He's being doing this for over twenty years and he shared his knowledge freely with us. He had a very engaging style mixing facts, stories and humour at a pace that never dragged nor did it overload us. We stopped at several viewpoints on the South Rim to admire the views and learn about the history of the area. We also had many opportunities to walk right up to the canyon's edge and gaze across at the North Rim opposite us. With the help of a telescope that Bob had brought with him we were also able to see down to the Colorado River nearly one mile below us.

I particularly enjoyed walking along the Trail of Time. Every three feet on this 3-mile trail represented one million years of geological time. Information boards and exhibits along the trail helped to unpack the geology. The sheer timescale of the story that we were told was staggering. It really did make me feel quite insignificant – my miniscule wheel marks on the surface of Mother Earth. My 61 years on this planet were represented by less than one thousandth of an inch on the trail. Quite a sobering thought. The Grand Canyon was everything I had hoped it would be and then some. Its sheer scale defies description, by me at least. I would really have liked to have seen the sunrise there as I am sure that the experience would have been an amazing one. By coincidence my eldest daughter, Katherine, was there at dawn about a week after me. Her description of what she experienced left me feeling that I had missed a great opportunity. Well, maybe one day...

After our rest day it was good to be back on the road and CV was rearing to go. As we rode out of Flagstaff I caught a glimpse of the San Francisco Peaks that define the landscape on the north side of the city. They are the remains of San Francisco Mountain which was a volcano until it collapsed following a spectacular eruption some 200,000 years ago. The highest mountain, the highest in the State of Arizona, is Humpreys Peak which rises to 12,600 feet. Before the eruption the parent San Francisco Mountain was another mile higher than today. There are some local sages who assert that another volcanic eruption is overdue!

The mountains here have been very important to the culture and spirituality of a number of American Indian tribes – the Navajo call them Dook'o'oosliid (the summit which never melts). The other major tribe in the area, the Hopi, named them Nuva'tukya'ovi (place of snow on the very top). Now the range is popular with skiers and there are a huge number of cycle trails to explore. Shortly before our visit, Flagstaff had been covered by several feet of snow but in today's sunshine you would never have guessed it.

Our regular quartet, David, Emil, Pete and I formed up pretty quickly as we left Flagstaff. Robin, one of the tour crew has christened us the 'Fab Four'. That had a nice ring to it! Pete accurately described today's stage to Holbrook as transitional, that is covering the greatest possible distance by the most direct route. Unfortunately, this meant that we were back on the interstate (I-40) for most of the day, although we were following the line of the historic Route 66. With a strong tailwind we made great speed, rolling along at 20–25 miles per hour. Shortly after joining the interstate I led us up what would normally be a very short, easy uphill stretch – almost too gentle to call a climb. As I was riding it I noticed that my breathing was getting slightly laboured and a quick peek at my Garmin revealed that we were at an altitude of 6,800 feet. With the massive open landscape all around us it is easy to forget how high we were – well, high for me compared to my normal terrain in East Anglia where I can ride at altitudes that are below sea level. Fortunately the route profile showed that over the next 50 miles we would gradually descend to about 5,000 feet.

Riding along the interstate was pretty boring. Today the shoulder was quite rough and gravelly – but still smoother than many of the minor roads I ride on back home. Riding the long straights where I could see the road stretching ahead for miles became almost hypnotic. To help pass the time I played a mind game. This involved looking at the mileage on my Garmin, then picking a distant landmark on the line of our route, maybe a water tower, or a radio mast or a tall building and guessing how far I was from it. Then when I reached the landmark I looked again at the mileage on my Garmin. I consistently underestimated the distances, sometimes by several miles.

When I got bored of that I sometimes tried to guess when I'd ridden a set distance, say 5 miles. I'm a bit better at this. What I don't do is count down the miles to the finish as I am riding along – that's a recipe for a headache! I do check the mileage remaining at each SAG though. The last SAG of the day is usually around 20 miles from the finish. Now in my mind, 20 miles is a short after-work ride. To have finished 'work' and be riding at 2pm was a pretty good feeling! But I'm in danger of getting ahead of myself here.

We reached the first SAG after 40 miles so that was a chance to break the monotony. Then it was more of the same for the next 20 miles to Winslow. About 2 miles from Winslow and in the full heat of the day, I had a rear wheel puncture (one of those evil thin wires from burst truck tyres) so that rang the changes. The Fab Four were great and helped me with the tube change so I was soon underway again and we arrived in Winslow shortly afterwards, accompanied by Robin and Mary from the tour crew. First up was a moment to play the tourist by getting the obligatory pic while 'Standing on The Corner in Winslow Arizona'. We actually took a lot of photos. Everyone had at least one solo shot, then there were numerous group photos, some taken by us and others taken by passers-by. I reckon if Jackson Browne and Glenn Frey, who wrote the song 'Take it Easy', got a dollar for every photo taken by 'their' corner they would have earned more than they did through song sales and publishing royalties. With the construction of the Interstate, Winslow, like many towns on the historic Route 66, has had to reinvent itself and get a new USP. 'That song' has proven too be the catalyst, though I have to say that based on what I saw of the town, success has been mixed.

Once we'd all posed on the corner we adjourned to a seemingly unremarkable nearby Mexican café, Las Marias, for an early lunch. Despite its plain appearance the food was delicious and after devouring a rather tasty bean enchilada I reluctantly set off again for the next leg of the interstate experience. By now the wind speed had picked up with gusts up to 40 miles per hour and it was blowing from the south, in other words we had a crosswind to contend with. This meant that the riding was pretty tough and staying upright required considerable concentration and strength. We rode along in a mini-echelon – in the time-honoured way that cyclists use to cope with sidewinds.

After another 25 miles we turned off for the second SAG of the day and to experience one of those slightly bizarre sights that we encountered every so often. At this morning's route rap we had been told that we would 'Ride the Rabbit' which had got me slightly worried. Was this some sort of novel Arizona custom? Was it legal? Would I rise to the challenge, whatever it was? These, and many other unmentionable thoughts had been playing on my mind for much of the day. Well readers, I needn't have worried. The Jack Rabbit Trading Post is one of the iconic sights on Route 66 – it even has its own named exit on the interstate. And in case you're wondering, no, I didn't get arrested for riding the rabbit. It's a large fibre glass sculpture and that's what it was there for. Ride 'em cowboy!

Following our little entertainment it was more of the same – back on the interstate for the final drag to Holbrook and the end of today's stage. To help break the monotony I sometimes sing, and not always quietly, to myself! Today, I let rip with a verse or two of that eponymous Chuck Berry song. You know the one, don't you? Like Chuck I was certainly getting my kicks on Route 66. Why don't you sing a verse or two and get into our groove? Go on – I dare you!

That infernal sidewind didn't let up. If anything it swung around a tad so that I was riding into it slightly. We stopped at a Dairy Queen fast food outlet for a milkshake about half a mile before our hotel. When I got off CV, my right hand was numb and my forearm was quite sore from the effects of holding the handlebars and fighting the wind. CV seemed untroubled by the experience. But rest assured, within an hour of arriving at the hotel and after washing my kit in the shower I felt great again. Our hotel, the Lexington Inn, didn't provide dinner so industrial quantities of pizza were ordered in for us. Fuel, rather than food. As there was no bar either I popped over the road to the gas station to buy some beer for The Fab Four and the attendant commented that he had sold more beer this evening than he had in the rest of the year so far. Yep, the cyclists are in town. Bring it on!

Stage 9: Tuesday 22 May, Holbrook to Gallup (94 Miles)

Holbrook, where we stayed overnight has had a fairly colourful history as a wild-west town. The most notorious incident occurred in 1887 when the Sheriff, Perry Owens confronted four members of a local family, the Blevins, who had been involved in a number of crimes, including stealing horses which was punishable by hanging. In the ensuing gunfight, Sheriff Perry emerged unscathed, one of the Blevin brothers, and a friend were killed; the other brother was wounded. This elevated the Sheriff's reputation as a man not to be trifled with. Today, Holbrook is a rather more sedate place and from what I saw, existed principally as a transport hub. The constant flow of trucks and trains and the large number of motels and budget hotels, diners and fast food outlets, with the associated services all point to this.

We left Holbrook on another transitional stage; another day of interstate riding on I-40. It's starting to get a bit dull and I resolved, when I'm back home after the tour, to get my atlas out and work out a route that involves no interstate riding. I will be interested to see how much this adds to the total mileage. Once again the massive desert landscape defined the riding. Much of the land was uninhabited though from time to time we passed small, ramshackle houses – some abandoned, others still lived in. It struck me that it must be really hard scratching a living here. All around were signs highlighting that we were in Navajo territory.

Our second SAG was at an Indian Gift Shop but I didn't see anything that enticed me to buy a souvenir. Well, that isn't quite true. I did spot a full-size fibreglass replica of a tribal chief complete with a magnificent headdress. I thought it would make a good addition to my décor back home and it would certainly be a talking point. Sadly, that thirty-pound weight limit the organisers had placed on our luggage stopped the idea in its tracks. Without that I am sure that 'The Chief' would have been happy to have had a lift on my crossbar to the end of the stage. So I settled instead for a cooling ice-cream. Just before setting off again I checked my rear wheel to discover that it was going soft. Closer inspection revealed that the tube had been pierced by two of those infernal metal shards from burst truck tyres so a tube change was needed.

It seemed that almost everyone had at least one puncture today and some more than one. A tally later that evening suggested that the total puncture count for the day was close to 40! This was one of the major downsides of riding on the interstate. And replacing a tube in the heat of full sun with dust and exhaust fumes swirling around as trucks thunder past is no fun at all. Quite the opposite.

But despair not. There was an upside. And a big one it was too. At one of our innumerable puncture stops I stepped back for a moment and looked on. The rider with the puncture was surrounded by six others, each of whom was helping their friend to get going again as quickly as possible. The group was working like a well drilled Formula One motor racing pit crew. Everyone had a part to play and everyone played their part. This supportive ethos has been developing organically over the last few days. As we progress it has started to become one of the tour's defining characteristics. Riders supporting each other – sometimes by action, sometimes with a friendly world of encouragement or a joke, or often just a simple look or nod to say: "I know where you're at; I'm there with you." Standing on the shoulder at the edge of a hot, dusty, busy interstate it struck me that I was observing a masterclass in team building. Businesses often spend large sums of money and engage consultants in an attempt to develop their teams. Well, maybe bike riding is an answer. As the tour progressed eastwards the level of support amongst us, the riders, continued to grow and eventually surpassed that provided by the tour organisers. There was a level of understanding and empathy between us that I have rarely felt on other tours. As I wrote earlier, good routes make good tours. Great tours are made by great riders.

After riding across Arizona for the last 6 days and 400 miles we finally crossed the state line into New Mexico. Yet again I felt a sense of being overwhelmed by the sheer size and scale of this country. New Mexico bills itself as The Land of Enchantment and I was eager to see how this manifested itself. Crossing the state line also marked another change as we passed out of the Pacific Time Zone and rode into the Mountain Time Zone. That meant that we had 'lost' an hour today.

Approaching Gallup, our destination for the day, Pete and I, together with Robert and Robin, two of the tour support crew, pulled into a Taco Bell outlet for a spot of end of stage refreshment. Robin very kindly bought us all tacos – CV had her first one, enjoyed it and said: "Big thanks Robin". Then it was a short spin down to our hotel for the night – the Comfort Inn. Soon after arriving I realised that I had left my Camelbak containing my tools, a credit card and some cash at the Taco Bell so I had to ride back to collect it, adding an extra 10 miles to the day's total. Doh!

Today was both a happy day and a sad one. Navi, one of the tour riders found out this morning that she had qualified for medical school. Compared to the rest of the team she is relatively new to cycling and seemed to be really enjoying herself. Bob, who was one of the more experienced riders on the tour, left us today. Bob was best described as a 'character' and I knew that I was going to miss his friendly greetings. We celebrated with beer and cake – as all good cyclists do! Chapeau Bob and Chapeau Navi!

Stage 10: Wednesday 23 May, Gallup to Grants (66 Miles)

At last, a day with very little interstate riding. A reason to celebrate, or so I thought. Instead we were going to step back in time and spend some of the day riding along the iconic Route 66. I was really looking forward to this for several reasons. It was a chance to experience a slice of American history. As part of my pre-tour research I had read a few books about journeys along this historic road and I have also watched a few documentaries. One of my favourites was the film made by the Big Yin, the Scottish comedian Billy Connolly. He has a wonderful talent for getting the best out of the people he met on his travels. And his trademark and sometimes self-deprecating humour meant that he never took himself too seriously. It's well worth watching. The soundtrack CD is pretty good too.

Getting out of Gallup was fairly straightforward although there was quite a lot of traffic with people going to work. I could feel CV shudder slightly as we approached the intersection for the interstate then she relaxed noticeably as we rode past the onramp and onto Route 66. I think I even heard her give a little whoop of joy! I was distracted at the time as my Garmin was misbehaving and wasn't loading the route correctly. After a few attempts to reload the route I gave up. Today wouldn't involve much navigation and the route notes had all the information I needed.

Once out into the countryside I could see the road stretching invitingly ahead of me. With virtually no other traffic this was a great time to enjoy the sights and sounds of the countryside we were passing through. For the first time for several days it was even quiet enough to hear the birds singing which only added to my feelings of elation. With the road stretching into the far distance I thought I could go off the front and grab a longshot photo of The Fab Four. So I changed up a couple of gears, stood up and gave it all I'd got – like a sprinter. As I shot past them I heard a couple of confused shouts. "Photo opp" I replied. I later discovered they didn't hear what I had said and thought I might have been stung by a bee! Anyway I rapidly opened up a gap of about 400 yards before reaching a gentle incline, about one per cent. Suddenly I realised that my breathing was laboured and then I remembered that we were still at 6,500 feet. Looking back over my shoulder I could see that the gap was now holding, not increasing. I pulled over, extracted the camera from my back pocket and just as I had got it focussed The Fab Four passed me. But I did get a nice shot of a long, straight and empty road behind them!

After 16 miles unfortunately Route 66 was no longer available and we had to turn on to the dreaded I-40 for the next 10 miles. The good news was that none of The Fab Four had a puncture. The bad news was this was probably the worst stretch of interstate we had ridden to date. It made the California Cobbles seem like the smooth surface of an indoor wooden cycling track. The shoulder was very rough, to the point of being unrideable so we had to sit between the white line marking the side of the carriageway and the vibration strip which warns vehicles when they drift off the unusually busy carriageway towards the shoulder. Riding on a strip of tarmac about 6 inches wide with heavy lorries passing at speed about 18 inches away from my shoulder was quite unnerving. Fortunately we covered the 10 miles without incident and eventually turned off I-40 for the day's first SAG.

The SAG was at another landmark on the tour. We had now reached the Continental Divide at an altitude of 7,275 feet. This is a mountainous hydrological line that runs from Alaska in the north through the Rockies and thence down through the Andes to Tierra Del Fuego. Water landing on the western side flows into the Pacific and on the Eastern side into the Atlantic.

In the time-honoured tradition, I snuck off behind the store and stood astride the divide to conduct a little experiment. Now, some of my own waters are making their way to the two oceans simultaneously!

Once out of the SAG it was back onto Route 66 for the rest of the day. This was really enjoyable. We were sandwiched between the interstate on our right and a railway line on our left. The road itself was very quiet – so quiet that we could ride two and sometimes even three abreast. With virtually no traffic, it was a time for looking around and admiring the scenery. Away to the right across the desert was a range of hills about 10 miles away which looked like they were covered in forest. A couple of miles away on our left was a line of picturesque ochre and red sandstone cliffs and bluffs which had been weathered into some amazing shapes. In front of us was a range of mountains, the tail end of the Rockies which rose to over 10,000 feet.

If the splendour of the scenery wasn't enough, we were passed by a succession of freight trains. Each one was at least a mile long and pulled by up to five diesel engines often with another couple of engines at the back. They chugged along at around 40 miles per hour and took several minutes to pass us by. I tried counting the number of container wagons on one and lost count at about 65! Several of the trains had two layers of containers, one above the other which added to their sense of power. A couple of the trains were carrying fully-loaded lorry trailers which to me seemed a great way to reduce the volume of long-distance traffic on the highways.

As we made our way along the road the wind turned so that we began to ride into quite a strong headwind. To beat the wind we formed a chain-gang and did some through and offs, with each of us taking a turn on the front for about a mile before peeling off to rest at the back. At one stage when the road changed direction so that the wind was blowing onto our shoulders, we formed an echelon to maximise our efficiency. After several days of being together our formation riding was now almost instinctive. What this also meant was that we could sustain a good pace in spite of the wind, so that we arrived at the stage finish in Grants by early afternoon.

As we rode in, Pete spotted a rather large and magnificent Route 66 road sign, so we pulled over for a photo. Adjacent to the sign in a large grass area I saw a group of people carefully placing small white wooden crosses in the ground. I strolled over to find out more and discovered that this was a civic group who were preparing for Memorial Day on 28 May. This is a federal holiday to commemorate the people who died while serving in the country's armed forces, rather like Remembrance Sunday in the UK. As I stood and reflected on the row upon row of white crosses I found it quite moving to think that in a small town of about 10,000 people so many have given their lives.

Then it was a short ride to our hotel which, despite our early arrival, was ready and welcoming. As I wheeled my bike into my room there on the bed were my two bags. This is one of those small details that makes such a difference at the end of a day's riding. Finding my kit ready and waiting for me instead of having to lug bags and bike along unfamiliar corridors makes it all so easy. All I then have to do is unearth my sponge bag and clean clothes and dive into the shower so that I can wash off the road dust and grime and become a human again! Today was a day to reflect and a day to celebrate. And another day closer to the Atlantic. Will I arrive there before my pee does? When I switched off my Garmin, which, despite the navigational freeze, had carried on recording my ride, I noticed that today I had ridden 66 Miles on Route 66. Coincidence or what?

Stage 11: Thursday 24 May, Grants to Albuquerque (79 Miles)

There was a distinct chill in the air this morning as we lined up for the stage start outside our hotel in Grants. This was also quite a poignant moment for The Fab Four as this was the last time that we would be riding with David. He would be heading home to Maine the following day as he was only able to ride the first part of the tour. I have really enjoyed riding with him over the last couple of weeks. He has a very laid back, almost laconic personality but as I got to know him, I realised that he is both a very generous person and has a razor-sharp sense of humour. He owns a brewery so he has played an important role in ensuring that our post ride refreshments were of the highest standards. The Fab Four will never be quite the same without him.

We were really pleased not to be riding on the interstate today, at least for the first part of the ride. We were soon back on to Route 66 and heading east on a very quiet road. Quiet enough to once again ride two and three abreast and have some great conversations and a bit of banter. Around us, the hills and bluffs seemed much closer and we marvelled at the magnificent scenery. This was a landscape that was very familiar to me from the countless Westerns that I have watched on TV and in the cinema. In a few places I almost expected to see John Wayne, Kirk Douglas or Spencer Tracy (that dates me) leading a posse after some bandits or outlaws. The rock faces even hinted at the perfect place to stage an ambush.

As I rode along Route 66 I was struck by how much the fortunes of people who lived alongside the highway have changed with the arrival of the interstate. I passed several ranch entrances which hinted at economic activity beyond their gates. I was also struck by the number of abandoned and derelict properties and stores which had closed because of a lack of passing trade. There were still quite a few properties where people were making some sort of a living – a small roadside convenience store or a business supporting the local farming activity such as a blacksmith or an ironmonger. The most vibrant seemed to be the public service facilities such as the post offices and a school that I passed which literally appeared to be in the middle of nowhere. Occasionally we passed through small communities and hamlets.

Once such place was Laguna, which was originally known by its native name of 'Tó Láni' which means 'Much Water'. Archaeological records suggest that the area had been inhabited for at least 10,000 years. The Spanish arrived here in 1540 and after a turbulent time when control of the area oscillated between the indigenous peoples and the Spaniards, the latter eventually built the new Pueblo in 1699, naming it San Jose de a Laguna (St. Joseph of the Lake), and subsequently shortened it to Laguna. The term 'Pueblo' originally referred to communities of Native Americans. The Spaniards also used it to describe communities housed in apartment structures built of stone, adobe mud, and other local materials. Today with a school, churches, stores and a post office, Laguna is a centre for a wide area.

Despite the relatively busy sense that I had while passing through Laguna I found it quite sad to be riding in an area where several of the small communities and traditional farm holdings seemed to be struggling and slowly disappearing or dissolving back into the desert sands. Such is the price of progress, hastened by the interstate. I may have misread the signals but I can only tell it like I saw it.

After riding for about 30 miles we arrived at the day's first SAG in a service area. This was a signal that we would be back on the interstate for a spell. With some small pies on offer, CV opted for what she told me was a rather tasty peach number! Just as we were about to set off David discovered that his rear tyre was soft so a tube change was needed. I was impressed that after fitting a new inner tube he then patched the old one! Most riders usually discard them. He said that as he was riding large tyres (32mm; I'm using 28mm) he preferred to use larger tubes compared to the smaller size that I had fitted and he was happy to repair them. Once David was ready we set off along the interstate (I-40) which this time fortunately had a wide and generally smooth shoulder. There was still quite a lot of debris though which led to Emil having a rear wheel puncture after about 5 miles. The rest of The Fab Four again rose to the occasion and Emil was soon 'good to go'. Fortunately we completed the remaining 25 miles of interstate riding without any further incident and arrived at the second SAG stop where we refreshed ourselves with ice creams at a Dairy Queen outlet.

Then it was back on the road with a four-mile hot drag uphill. Approaching the crest which I had been riding towards for what seemed like forever (it was actually 23 minutes according to my Garmin) I was amused to see a sign reading 'Lost Horizon'. In the distance were the mountains, the tail end of the Rockies. Cresting the climb we rode down and over I-40 onto a magnificent downhill straight which ran all the way into Albuquerque. With a straight and a clear road ahead this was a great opportunity to get down low over the crossbar and freewheel – I got up to 38 miles per hour before I had to stop at the red traffic lights. The day's final landmark was a crossing of the Rio Grande which over the course of nearly 1,800 miles (it's the fourth longest river in the US) flows from Colorado to the Gulf of Mexico. We paused to take a photograph of the sign at the start of the river crossing but had to move on swiftly because out of nowhere a vagrant, who looked like a Zombie, appeared and with wildly waving arms started coming menacingly towards us. We made it to safety on the far side of the bridge where Pete took a picture of me posing by holding CV aloft above my head. We do like a bit of posing!

A fast ride through the outskirts of Albuquerque brought us to our hotel for the night. Dinner this evening was a rather special event as we said our goodbyes to David and also to Lawrence who were leaving us. A couple of short impromptu speeches commemorated the occasion. David absolutely hit the nail on the head when he reiterated my view that what makes a good ride is the route you ride; what makes a great ride are the people you ride with. Chapeau David, The Fab Four are no more; long live The Fab Four!

Stage 12: Friday 25 May, Albuquerque to Santa Fe (67 Miles)

With a tinge of sadness The Fabs, as we have re-christened ourselves sans David, rolled out of Albuquerque under blue skies with the promise of a hot day ahead. I could sense that we were all going to miss David's company on the road. More positively, today was the first day for some time that we wouldn't be riding on the interstate at all. Hooray! The theme of the first part of today's ride was climbing, rising 2,000 feet over the first 20 miles. This was a long, steady climb on a wonderfully smooth surface, ideal for spinning up. Starting at an altitude of 5,000 feet this was not a time for heroics but instead one for setting a measured pace and maintaining a steady breathing cycle. Ahead and to our side we could see the mountains rising up to over 10,000 feet. In the clear air, once again the views were great.

We rode on the Turquoise Trail, a scenic route set in 15,000 square miles of land. To put that in context that's ten times bigger than my home county of Suffolk! The Trail is named after the blue-green rocks originally mined by the Pueblo people over 1,000 years ago. Prized as a precious stone, the turquoise is widely used in jewellery. The area was also the site of a big gold rush in 1825, pre-dating the more famous California Gold Rush by several years. Traces of the mining activity were visible as we rode along the road. It is a hugely popular tourist area and we were passed by several groups of motorcyclists riding their Hogs (Harley Davidsons) with their distinctive rumble and roar. We also saw lots of large, truck sized recreational vehicles and camper vans. Today was the start of a holiday weekend – Memorial Day is on Monday – so lots of people were making the most of it.

After 35 miles we arrived at our first and only SAG of the day at Henderson's Store, which sells Southwestern American Indian jewellery, rugs and pottery. I had a quick look around inside and marvelled both at the items on display and the high prices. A pair of old assay scales, which had been magnificently restored with the brass gleaming, were the centrepiece of the display. There were lots of old black and white photographs including one of the store's founder sitting in a rocking chair on the front step. I could almost imagine him surveying the trail expectantly, while chewing on some tobacco and awaiting the next group of passing travellers.

Once we were refreshed we descended to the small town of Madrid, which is pronounced Ma-adrid, and not like the Spanish capital. This was a lovely little ramshackle place with lots of small galleries, shops and eateries. Until 1954 coal mining was the main activity here. Now it is a popular tourist destination and has quite a boho, hippy-like feel to it, once you get past the bustle and noise of the visitors. We stopped for lunch at a roadside restaurant, sitting outdoors under the trees and watching all of life pass us by. In the hot sun I was reminded of Pooh Bear – "sometimes I sits and thinks and sometimes I just sits." Today I just sat and tuned out – wonderful! The homemade burger and the cold beer gave this the perfect ambience. I could have happily stayed put all afternoon

Sadly, I had places to go and people to see so we broke the reverie and headed off on the final 20-mile leg of the day. I was glad of the initial downhill run as with a longer than usual lunch break my legs had stiffened up. Also, the after-effects of sitting in the sun had made me feel quite drowsy. Or maybe it was the beer? Whatever, it meant that I found it quite difficult to concentrate and I left it to CV to take charge. I think she may have muttered a few expletives about me under her breath! Fortunately, after a few miles of gentle spinning, bike and rider were reunited in perfect harmony and we completed the stage without incident.

Approaching Santa Fe I could see a massive building ahead of me on my right. This turned out to be Santa Fe County Adult Correctional Facility (i.e. the jailhouse). Their mission, and I quote, is:

> *"To provide expedient, professional, and ethical quality service in partnerships with the community to create a safe and secure environment for the citizens of Santa Fe County and all others entrusted in our custody. We are committed to serving with integrity, cooperation and concern for the welfare of others. Our standards are excellence and our model of success is teamwork."*

Wow, that's a mouthful. As I passed the site I was amused to see a large road sign instructing motorists not to pick up hitchhikers! This was clearly not the place to linger so I upped the cadence and sped past.

Arriving in Santa Fe I had a mission to undertake. For the last couple of days CV's rear brake had become very spongy to the point of being almost ineffective. Riding mountainous descents with only one fully working brake is not something we wanted to do. I guessed some air had got into her hydraulics and the brake needed bleeding. Although I had brought a bleed kit and spare hydraulic fluid with me, ideally I wanted to get it fixed in a bike shop in case there was an underlying issue such as a leaky hose. With a quick spot of giggling on my iPhone I headed off with Pete in tow to Bike N' Sport on the other side of town. They were absolutely brilliant. Despite pitching up unannounced Tony Ferrari and his mechanic, whose name sadly I didn't get, came to my rescue. My decision to visit the professionals was a wise one when they discovered that the alloy Allen key slot in the bleed cap on the top brake levers was rounded and couldn't be undone. This was apparently a known issue with this version of Shimanono levers and they had a stock of replacements on order. After about 20 minutes with a bit of a workaround CV was fully functional again and I was both a happy and hugely reassured rider! CV was pretty happy too as she had been getting a bit fed up with stopping on her front brake only. Considering that I arrived unannounced out of nowhere late on a Friday afternoon their response was beyond outstanding. So Chapeau team Bike N' Sport. And if any readers happen to be in the area with a bike problem this has to be the go-to place for a fix. But perhaps, unlike me, a phone call first would be appreciated.

Then it was back to the hotel for a shower and dinner. We have now covered over 9,800 miles and Santa Fe was our second rest day. I was looking forward to exploring the city. The prospect of spending two nights in the same bed was pretty enticing too. After a good night's rest I gave CV the once over and was delighted to discover that her brakes were fully pumped. No leakages. CV was pretty happy too and was even happier when I said she could have a lazy day and go back bed.

The day had ended on a sad note when I discovered that Robert, one of the tour crew had left the tour earlier that day. Although no one was saying anything about the reasons for his departure I sensed that it wasn't entirely of his own making. I was more than a little surprised at this news since, like many other riders, I had really enjoyed Robert's company and his good humour and willingness to help and encourage us was a real motivator. He resonated with the dynamics and ethos that the riders and I shared. I was very disappointed that I didn't get an opportunity to say goodbye to my new friend and I found it very strange that no mention was made of his departure by the tour organisers, at least in my earshot. It was as if he had been whitewashed out of our script. Although I didn't know it at the time, later in the year I would meet Robert again and we would enjoy another ride together. I also discovered that another of the tour crew had parted company with us earlier on. Louis, who I don't think I actually spoke to, had also been whitewashed. Had I realised at the time what was happening I might have thought that I was a participant in some sort of bizarre reality game show – or worse!

Most of the places we have stayed in so far on the tour tend to be located on the edge of the town or city and they all looked and felt the same – as if they have been made from a kit. A sort of concrete Lego set. They were purely functional serving the needs of overnighters, travellers, salespeople and so forth. Fine as far as they went but they lacked character and ambience. I don't wish to sound overly critical here; they were ideal for this sort of tour, easily accessible on the edge of the town or city. Totally predictable in their standardised offer so no nasty surprises awaited us. Nothing to be worried about or to get in the way of the essential start and end of day routines. What this meant though was that, with a few exceptions, I probably got a totally skewed view of the towns and cities we've stayed in. I was delighted to have the chance to go and feel the pulse and take the temperature of Santa Fe which, according to my pre-tour research offered a lot of history and culture to be investigated and enjoyed.

Pete had a couple of contacts here, friends of friends of his brother in law, who had got in touch with him and they had offered to meet us and introduce us to the delights of the city.

Foregoing the usual hotel breakfast fare we moseyed on down to the Plaza in the heart of Santa Fe to meet Dan and Phyllis for brunch at the Famous Plaza Café. Over a wonderful fry-up we got to know them and quickly felt at ease. Once we had completed our introductions we had a look around the Plaza which was very busy – there was a parade of custom cars taking place which drew lots of spectators. We also had a look in a local museum as well as visiting an indoor market with Indian art on sale. Dan and Phyllis then left us to our own devices and, on their recommendation we walked up Canyon Road to look the dozens of art galleries there.

This was a fantastic area with more small galleries than I could shake a stick at. I could easily have spent a couple of days looking around and even then probably have only scratched the surface. I enjoyed talking to several of the artists and gallery owners along the way. I especially enjoyed chatting to Kat Livengood an artist who photographs wildlife, particularly horses in the wonderful landscapes of the West. I was captivated by her black and white work where the grain, textures and tones of her images totally captured the sense of place. The landscapes evoked powerful memories of what I had seen and felt over the last few days. Sadly, I don't have the words to fully express the feelings that Kat's work stirred in me, but I felt privileged to have had an opportunity to see it. As someone who has spent much of my life working outdoors conserving the natural environment I was delighted too to learn that Kat donated a proportion of her income to conserving and supporting wild animal welfare. Sadly, all good things must come to an end so after meeting Dan and Phyllis for a farewell pizza and beer we were back in our hotel for an early night before resuming the tour.

SANTA FE TO ABILENE : 9 DAYS, 686 MILES

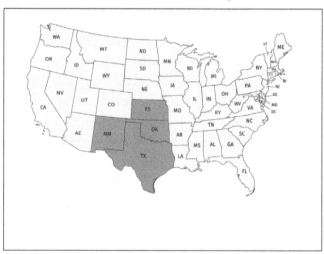

4. AN ENCOUNTER WITH SOME HOOKERS!

Stage 13: Sunday 27 May, Santa Fe to Las Vegas (74 Miles)
The sun was shining as we left Santa Fe bound for Las Vegas, New Mexico, not the other more famous one. Going to 'the other one' would have involved riding a few hundred miles in the opposite direction and almost back to California. I've highlighted this point because several people I spoke to looked askance at me when I mentioned that we were going to Las Vegas today and I had to give them a little lesson in geography. These people included a surprising number of New Mexicans, if that's the correct term for them. Considering that our Las Vegas was only 75 miles down the road it did seemed a bit odd. So readers, I wouldn't want you to make the same mistake! Rather like the start of our previous stage we began with a long steady climb up to 7,500 feet over the next 20 miles. Once again my breathing was feeling the effects of the altitude – having to work a bit harder to get sufficient oxygen to fuel the effort of riding uphill. Nothing significant and I certainly wasn't suffering from altitude sickness but just enough to make the effort slightly harder than I had anticipated. In this massive open landscape it was very easy to forget that we were riding at quite a high altitude.

In a complete contrast to previous days we had something new to admire today – trees! Most of today was in the Santa Fe National Forest and Pecos National Park. The Forest covers an area of about 1.6 million acres with 1,000 miles of trails for visitors to explore by bike, on foot or on horseback. The area is rich in wildlife and nearly one third of the Park is designated as wilderness. My forester's eye was inevitably drawn to the tree species – pinyon and ponderosa pines, Douglas fir, oak, aspen and juniper to name a few. Overall the forest seemed to me to be in pretty good shape with evidence of active management, some past fire damage and several examples of excellent habitat conservation. If only I had the time I could have spent several days exploring the area. Maybe I should come back...?

As we passed through the town of Pecos I was reminded of the infamous Judge Roy Bean, a saloon keeper and justice of the peace, who anointed himself as the 'Law West of the Pecos'. His courtroom was his saloon and he used to dole out his version of justice while seated on a whisky barrel. It is probably best to describe his life as 'colourful'. Several books have been written and TV series and films featuring the judge – most with a large helping of artistic licence. As one of my blog followers was quick to point out, The Judge's Pecos is in Texas and I was a long way out with my geography. But what of 'my Pecos'?

Rather like Laguna on the other side of Santa Fe, people have been living here since the eighth century. The Pecos Pueblo played an important role in the local economy until at least 1450 when the Spanish Conquistadors arrived looking for the fabled Seven Cities of Gold (Cibola). They were followed by some settlers with their livestock and ten Franciscan monks in tow. The monks settled down, building a mission church. Over the next several hundred years ownership and control of the area ebbed and flowed between the indigenous peoples and the Spaniards. In the late nineteenth century, the area became a mining centre, principally for copper but also for gold, silver, lead and zinc. More recently, in 1948 some Trappist monks from Rhode Island established a new monastery here but they then moved to Oregon in 1955 after selling the monastery to some Benedictine monks. Now the site acts as a retreat for individuals and groups., Most of the people living here these days commute to Santa Fe for their work. Although it was only a relatively small community I found it fascinating to learn about some of the history and the role that the Catholic Church has played in communities like this up and down this land.

With a tailwind for most of the day we made excellent progress – at one point I looked down at my Garmin to see that CV and I were spinning along easily at 33 mph. I was barely turning her pedals. There was only one SAG today at 46 miles. Just as we were about to leave there was a large pop followed by the hiss of air. Poor Emil had suffered yet another rear wheel puncture – and he wasn't even on the bike at the time! No matter, The Fabs swung into action, a new tube was swiftly installed, and we were all underway pretty quickly. Ah, the benefits of team working! The last leg of the day crossed what seemed like a never-ending succession of rolling hills. None was particularly long or excessively steep but there were a lot of them. On some of the downhills CV and I were able to ride at over 40 miles per hour. And one or two of the uphill stretches were steep enough to get me changing down to CV's granny ring to get a low enough gear for the ascent. One of the things I've discovered that my Garmin does is that it counts the number of gear changes I do with my Shimanono Di2 electronic gears. For the record, I shifted the rear cassette 758 times today and the front one 30 times. Did you need to know that? Probably not. And while I'm telling you about the technology I'd like to confirm that my brakes were fully operational – the guys at Bike N' Sport in Santa Fe have done CV and me proud. Going downhill knowing that we've got maximum braking capability should we need it, is a very satisfying feeling. Going downhill fast, without worrying about braking, is even more satisfying!

We had made such good time on this 74-mile stage that we rolled in very early to Las Vegas. There was only one thing to do and we headed for the old part of town and sought out the historic Plaza Hotel. The hotel, which was originally known as 'The Belle of the Southwest', opened in 1882 and claimed to be the fanciest hotel in all of New Mexico. We sat outside the beautifully restored building on the front terrace watching the townspeople passing by. A visit to the restroom gave me an opportunity to have a look around the interior which had also been beautifully restored. The ballroom was spectacular. This was a hotel that oozed old-world charm and elegance. A cold beer, a massive and very tasty meatloaf burger and chips more than replenished the calories that my Garmin told me I'd burnt today. If you must know 3,625 calories. The Garmin is so clever it can probably tell me what I should eat next week on Tuesday! Then it was time to head for another Lego kit hotel – this time of the Best Western variety. Arriving there I was very tempted to turn around and get a room in the Plaza.

Oh, I nearly forgot a bit of good news. When I logged onto the Interweb in the hotel I found out that the Froomedog had won the Giro D'Italia. What a fantastic achievement. I can't wait to watch the highlights…

Stage 14: Monday 28 May, Las Vegas to Tucumcari (110 Miles)

Today was a big day for several reasons as you will discover when you read on. We left Las Vegas in the usual cool early morning air. The weather forecast was telling us that today was going to be hot and within half an hour I could feel the temperature rising. The route notes gave an indication of what we were going to face on the 110-mile stage. The key words were 'No restrooms or services for 74 miles'. Written in bold which was usually a clue for some pretty serious hazards along the route. It seemed that today's comfort breaks in the undergrowth might involve a rattlesnake check…!

Like our last two stages, we left Las Vegas heading upwards. Unlike the last two stages the ascent was very gentle – almost imperceptible. We were still at 6,500 feet so my lungs got their early morning workout. One thing I noticed immediately was the greenness of the vegetation so I guessed there must be marginally more rainfall here. I did see more damp watercourses and even a few streams with water which reinforced my thinking. This was cattle country and what country it was. Emil, who I was riding with at the start said it reminded him of being at sea – vast oceans of scrub grass stretching for miles in every direction. I spotted a couple of buzzards circling above the roadside looking for breakfast, but no albatrosses.

As is often the case when I'm riding on good roads with few hazards or traffic, my mind tends to wander in random directions. Emil's comment triggered vague memories of some lines from Coleridge's Rhyme of the Ancient Mariner:

"The fair breeze blew, the white foam flew
The furrow followed free;
We were the first that ever burst
Into that silent sea."

I tried to sing the lines that I could remember to the tune of Jerome Moross's soundtrack to the film 'The Big Country'. Now readers, bear with me. This might seem a pretty avant-garde thing to do or even rather eccentric behaviour but what I'm trying to convey here is what I was seeing and how it made me feel in my heart. Riding through some amazing territory, the sweeping strings and pulsating brass of the soundtrack just seemed so right. Today I felt like a pioneer, exploring a vast new landscape, soaring along just above the tarmac like the albatross over the ocean. The long, long straight roads punctuated with gently rolling hillocks were just so invigorating.

In seemingly no time at all we reached the first SAG and I was snapped out of my reverie. The SAG marked an important milestone on our journey east. We had completed the first 1,000 miles of the tour. A landmark moment and I was thrilled to see the joy, happiness and sense of achievement on the faces of my fellow riders. Well done us! I was so happy that I even tried reprising my Big Country Albatross song. Fortunately, I don't think anyone heard me!

With an air of satisfaction we rolled out of the SAG and continued on our way. At around the 35-mile mark we swung round a bend and, totally unexpectedly, the most magnificent view to the plains below opened up in front of us. This marked the start of a stupendous descent, dropping more than 1,000 feet over the next 5 miles. Enough of a drop in altitude to make my ears pop. Ahead of us lay a vast plain, framed by rust-red tree covered cliffs. And stretching away as far as my eyes could see, was the road we would be following. I experienced something that I'm not that well known for – speechlessness.

Reaching the bottom of the main descent we carried on along a smooth, gently downhill trajectory and with a good tailwind we spun along at an easy 20–25 mph. With a small uphill bump we reached the second SAG where we enjoyed an early alfresco lunch, including some tasty peanut butter and jelly sandwiches that Robin and Mary had prepared. Proper fuel for hungry cyclists. With the temperature building, it was hard to resist the temptation to linger and snag a second sarnie but we needed to press on and make as much progress as possible before the temperature rose too high.

Ahead of us lay something that several riders had mentioned in rather hushed tones over breakfast. A climb known as The Wall. No one seemed quite sure what it would involve and attempts to zoom in on the route profile didn't help much. Just the name seemed to be enough to invoke a tremor in some of my fellow riders. What was certain was that we would reach The Wall at mile 67. Pete and I were riding together at this point and ahead of us we could see some cliffs rising steeply, several hundred feet. Initially it seemed as if there was no way through the cliffs but eventually we could see a small cleft which we guessed was the way up. The terrain kept us guessing though and we continued to ride parallel to the cliffs. At the last moment the road turned ninety degrees to the right and took us into the cleft. I could see the road rearing up in front of us. However, it wasn't the steepness of the gradient that was the main challenge, it was the heat in the cleft. It was like riding into a furnace. As I rode up the narrow, very hot gorge I felt like a piece of toast in a toaster. Fortunately I popped out the top just nicely crisp and not burnt!

There was a nice surprise at the top because I met Phil, one of the riders, and Rick and his wife. Rick doubles as the tour mechanic. Phil was leaving the tour today, getting a lift home to Texas from Rick and wife. Rick would re-join us in about a week's time. I had chatted with Phil over breakfast that morning and he had seemed a bit subdued. Partly I sensed because he was leaving and also because he wasn't sure if he would have the time to ride as far as The Wall. Well he did and I was pleased to see him again, to shake his hand and wish him well. Chapeau Phil!

Emerging from the toaster, another 10 miles took us to the final SAG of the day and, that rare facility on today's stage – restrooms! The temperature had risen significantly now and my Garmin was reading 40°C (104°F) so I sought out a cooling ice cream and an ice-cold drink in the store. This was the hottest stage to date on the tour. The next 30 miles to Tucumcari were tough – long, rolling straights (one measured 10 miles), heat which collected in the furnaces between the hillocks, no shade and a hot sidewind. This was very much about riding within my limit, especially as we have another long stage tomorrow.

The final ascent in the full heat of the day was quite a challenge – physically and mentally. Pete and I eventually arrived at the top in Tucumcari with our water bottles empty and we descended on the first gas station we saw like crows landing on carrion, much to the amusement of the cashier and the apparent disgust of at least one customer who clearly wasn't a connoisseur of hot, sweaty, lycra-clad cyclists! Then it was a short pedal to our hotel where I rode straight in through the doors to the reception desk to check in. An ice bucket full of cold bottles of beer was ready and waiting. Then after I had whetted my whistle it was time for a shower. This had been quite a tough and long stage (110 miles) but a rewarding one. And once I'd showered I felt pretty good. No, I actually felt fabulous. So good that more words from the Rhyme came to me:

> *"Swiftly, swiftly flew the ship,*
> *Yet she sailed softly too:*
> *Sweetly, sweetly blew the breeze –*
> *On me alone it blew."*

Chatting with some of the other riders after dinner I learnt that much of the territory we had ridden through today featured in the film *No Country for Old Men* starting Javier Bardem, Josh Brolin and Tommy Lee Jones. So if you want to get a better feel for the scenery watch the film. I have and it's really rather good.

Stage 15: Tuesday 29 May, Tucumcari to Dalhart (96 Miles)

I can sum up today with three words: straight, flat, wind! Looking at my road atlas it appeared that the road between Tucumcari and Liberal, State Route 54, which was over 200 miles long and involved three days riding, was, one long continuous straight.

The route instructions were as simple as they get and along the lines of: "Leave hotel and turn left. Continue straight for 96 miles then turn right to arrive at hotel." I just hoped that the scenery along the route would provide sufficient stimulation to keep me awake.

As we left the La Quinta Inn in Tucumcari with 96 miles ahead of us to Dalhart I could see the road stretching endlessly to the horizon. And when I eventually reached the horizon point it stretched on again to the next horizon. And on to the next. Looking at the map on my Garmin the first 'straight' was 38 miles long before it curved gently on to another shorter straight which was 'only' 26 miles long. The terrain was generally flat with only a few fluctuations. This meant that I could see for at least 10 miles in every direction. The massive blue skies defined the feeling of today's ride. Living in the flat lands of East Anglia I am used to riding under big skies. They felt miniscule compared to what was above us today.

We also had to contend with a headwind today. I have an App (Windsock) that steals my Garmin data and does some clever stuff with the weather data to produce some fancy graphics. Looking at them in the hotel after completing the stage I discovered that I had been riding into a five to ten miles per hour headwind for 77 per cent of the day's ride. That may not seem particularly windy but be assured on those straights it certainly increased the workload, especially as I was still recovering from the previous day's 110-mile stage.

Today we recruited a session player into The Fabs. Greg comes from Tulsa, Oklahoma and was going to be with us for a couple of weeks. He was reasonably familiar with this territory – we'll be in Oklahoma tomorrow – and he has slotted in nicely. I say 'slotted in' because riding a pace line where we share out the work is the most efficient way to counter a headwind. With a road racing background, Greg was clearly a strong rider and well-used to through-and-offs. So, it was nice to be a quartet once more.

Rather like yesterday, there was a dearth of facilities along the route. We passed the last shop and restrooms at 25 miles. From then on we were reliant on the scheduled SAG stops at 30 and 65 miles on the stage. Riding on long roads in flat country can become quite monotonous so I am always on the lookout for 'excitement'. Anything to break the stupor. My reverie was broken by Pete's bike (a Specialised) which tried to have relations with CV and gave us both quite a shock. Fortunately, CV resisted the amorous advances of the Spesh and Pete and I were both able to maintain our dignity. Now I'm guessing readers, that some of you are wondering what the heck I'm writing about. Well, with a moment's loss of concentration our wheels collided, which in many situations can be devastating, frequently leading to road rash as riders and bikes slide along the tarmac. This time fortunately we all managed to stay upright.

The major landmark of the day was at 54 miles when we rode out of New Mexico and into The Lone Star State, Texas. There was a novel stone sign, complete with bullet holes, to welcome us. I'm claiming that the bullet holes are authentic; others may disagree!

As we rode into the state it became obvious that we were in cattle country. There was a distinct whiff of methane in the air. More tangibly, a succession of livestock trucks and trains passed us. A typical train had over 80 cattle wagons pulled by at least three locomotives. That implied one heck of a lot of steak. I am sure that you'd like to know that the Annual Texas Cattle Review for 2017 recorded 12.3 million head of cattle. That equates to just less than half a beast for every person in the state. Fascinating! Approaching Dalhart we passed a couple of gigantic cattle feeder stations where the livestock were brought for fattening before going to the slaughterhouse. I have never seen so many cows in one place in my life. As I stopped to take a picture the animals in the nearest pen gazed at me. I noticed that although the cattle were looking at me, their stares were empty-eyed and devoid of any sense of emotion. The sight of them standing in their pens awaiting their fate, was haunting. I was left thinking that I had stumbled across some sort of bovine concentration camp. But as one of the team commented later that evening, many of us enjoyed steak for dinner.

The other noticeable thing was the smell of methane in the air. So here's some trivia for you. On average one beef cow produces about 200 litres of methane per day. That is a lot of farting. Now, I can sense the inevitable question, so here's the answer. The average human farts between one half and two litres of methane per day. I bet you never thought you'd be reading stuff like this in a cycling tour book. And for the sake of completeness I have no idea what cyclists produce but based on my observations from the back of the pace line I'd say it's above the human average and probably less than that of a cow. Let's leave it there!!

Thinking about methane emissions helped to pass the time, a major goal for today. Combatting the mental stress of riding with relatively little stimulation was the toughest part of the day's ride. Arriving at Dalhart, which had the feel of a frontier town about it, gave me a huge lift so Pete and I adjourned to the nearest Dairy Queen to 'celebrate' with vanilla milkshakes. Unfortunately, the guy on the counter was operating solo and appeared to work at only one speed – reverse so we had to wait for our protein infusion a lot longer than we would have wished. Once we had recharged ourselves we headed over and checked in at our hotel. Rumours of steak for dinner were almost certainly true. And guess what? We've got more straight roads tomorrow. Would we break the 38-mile record? I hoped not…

Stage 16: Wednesday 30 May, Dalhart to Guymon (72 Miles)

Well, this seems to be habit forming; riding long, straight roads into the wind. Today's straight set a new record – 49 miles from the edge of Dalhart to the edge of Texhoma. All with a head or shoulder wind. The Fabs linked up with another group of riders to form an extended pace line which made the riding easier, much easier. Both physically and mentally. It was great to see us all riding in a line, sharing out the work efficiently. I occasionally have a tendency to go off the front a bit hard and have come to rely on Pete to keep me in check. Speeding up at the front of the line is considered poor etiquette so, fellow riders, if I was ever guilty of this then I apologise whole heartedly. My excuse is that without significant hills back home in East Anglia, I have got used to riding solo on long exposed roads.

I remember a story about the Belgian rider, Freddy Maertens, who twice won the World Professional Road Race Championships (in 1976 and 1981). Apparently, he used to get up in the early morning, have breakfast, get ready for a ride and then step outside. Next he would work out which way the wind was blowing and set off riding as hard as he could with a tailwind to help speed him along. He would ride flat out until he was totally knackered and then guess what? He would turn around and ride home into the headwind! Freddy had an extremely successful racing career as a pro – his achievements might have been even greater had his racing not coincided with the best years of Eddy Merckx. Freddy was one of my inspirations when I started riding seriously as a teenager and in my early twenties.

Anyway, let's get back to today's ride. From time to time a surprise pops up. Today, literally in the middle of nowhere, it was a gun-toting cowboy statue that stood 25 feet high. I have no idea why it was there and who, if anyone, it represented.

But it provided a good talking point and photo opportunity which helped to break the monotony. Leaving the gunslinger to his own devices we carried on along the road to the first SAG at Stratford, which I am guessing The Bard would probably have been underwhelmed by had he been able to drop in. As I discovered later this Stratford has nothing to do with the Bard. It was named after Stratford in West Virginia, the boyhood home of Robert E. Lee, the Confederate General. I have no idea why this connection was made.

Something unexpected happened to me at the SAG here. As I emerged from the restroom I bumped into the late Henry John Deutschendorf Jr's cousin. Yes, I did indeed. Who's that I hear you say? Well, Henry John Deutschendorf Jr. was better known as John Denver, the singer songwriter who tragically died while flying his experimental plane in 1997. I have no way of verifying the 'cousins' claim but my look into his eyes was returned with an unwavering stare and his handshake was Texas firm. Take me home, country roads.

At the 50-mile mark we left Texas. Our route north-east meant that we only clipped a corner of the state. Now we were into Oklahoma, the Sooner State. In 1889, the territory was opened to settlers. Thousands of people lined up on the border and, when the signal was given, they raced into the territory to claim their land. Some people went in early to claim their land and they became known as Sooners.

Subtly, the countryside around us was changing. Yes, there was still a lot of cattle territory but there were also signs of a new crop – wind turbines spinning gently and gracefully which evoked more memories of East Anglia, particularly Norfolk. I also had a vision or perhaps a hallucination of Don Quixote astride his horse Rocinante accompanied by his companion Sancho Panza, tilting at the windmills. It's the heat, readers! I'd probably been in the sun far too long. There were other clues

Celeste Victoria (CV) is born in Diss, Norfolk, 10 April

Wheel dip, Manhattan Beach, Los Angeles, 13 May

Desert heat on the road to Wickenburg, California, 16 May

The Fab Four (me, Pete, David and Emil), Yarnell, Arizona, 17 May

Approaching the Red Hills of Sedona, Arizona, 19 May

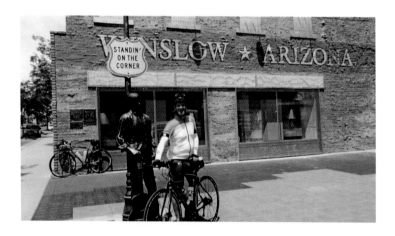

Taking it easy in Winslow, Arizona, 21 May

Team building, near Gallup, New Mexico 22 May

In the Land of Oz with Dorothy, Mary, Toto and Pete
doing his best Tin Man impression, Liberal, Kansas, 31 May

The Captain table dances with 25 miles to go to Kirksville, Missouri, 9 June

A sign of the times or for the times? Hillsboro, Indiana, 14 June

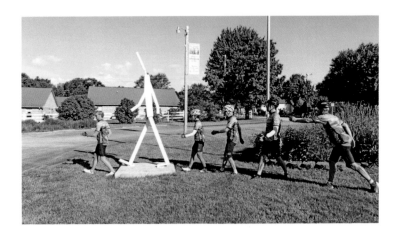

A spot of Madness on the road, Jamestown, Indiana, 15 June

Holding up Lincoln's funeral train, Cambridge City, Indiana, 16 June

Essential ice cream break with Pete, Cathy and Bruce, Utica,
New York, 25 June

Preparing for the final ride with my brothers, 'The Fabs', Pete and Emil,
Burlington, Massachusetts, 29 June

The tour team, Revere Beach, Boston, Massachusetts, 29 June

CV and I celebrate our achievement,
Revere Beach, Boston, Massachusetts, 29 June

to the nature of life in these parts. Huge billboards advertising drilling services, wind pumps and irrigation pipes all pointed to the importance of that most precious of resources. Water.

Despite the headwind at the start of the stage we covered the 70 miles to Guymon in record time. Guymon has branded itself as the 'Queen City of the Panhandle'. I'm not quite sure why though. More cynical folk use a rather different strapline: 'Home of the Most Lied–About Weather in the US'. If you're wondering how I know this then I'll let you into a little secret. Back in 1985 a guy called Jim Etter wrote an article in *The Oklahoman*. The title of his piece was 'Catchy Slogans Strive to Put Towns on Maps'. I quite like the sound of Elk City though. Their slogan proclaims: 'Get in Bed With Us Tonight'. Unfortunately it was a bit too far from our route for me to take up their generous offer. Instead I had to settle for another of those concrete Lego establishments. When I was tucked up in bed that evening I had a look at the route for the following day. Can you guess what I saw? Answers by email please.

Stage 17: Thursday 31 May, Guymon to Liberal (40 Miles)

The cast of today's story included a donkey, some hookers and a tin man! Today was also notable for a number of other reasons. First it was a short stage, only 40 miles across the Oklahoma Panhandle – look at the map and you'll understand the reference. Second it was the last leg of the seemingly never-ending 210-mile long straight which started two days ago. And lastly, and most importantly, a tailwind was a-blowin'. Yay! Last night we had a couple of minor thunderstorms, the second of which woke me at 1:30am with hail drumming against my bedroom window. I got up to have a look and the sky was being lit up by distant lightning flashes and I could see a few golf-ball sized hailstones bouncing in the parking lot which also had a small river flowing through it. Rather spectacular and unexpected entertainment. I was just glad it happened at night. Being caught in the open in that sort of weather would have been a challenge. By breakfast time, signs of the storm had largely disappeared with just the remnants of a few puddles in the parking lot and air which felt clean and clear but much more humid than yesterday.

This was a short day and we didn't set off until 9am but nevertheless I was still awake at my usual hour of 5:30am so I used the time to do some more background research on the Interweb about the next few stages of the tour. Unusually today, we all left the hotel together in one large group and headed down the road. I found myself alongside Emil and as we wound it up together we progressed right through the group becoming the leaders on the road. With the aid of the wind and on yet more smooth tarmac we were soon zipping along effortlessly at nearly 25 miles per hour. What fun! As we whizzed along I spotted my first nodding donkey pumping oil or gas, which like all the others I saw today, was asleep. Nevertheless the silhouette of that distinctive solitary beam against the skyline was, for me, a memorable sight. The countryside in this part of Oklahoma is big and expansive. But it is also subtly different and has a more managed feel to it. This is very much cattle country with large ranges of grass stretching in every direction. How I longed to be able to stand about ten to twenty feet off the ground and gaze into the distance. That would have really given me the chance to properly appreciate the scale of the place.

As I rode along I found myself reflecting on the last three days riding in these flatlands. What I saw has reminded me of the constant tussle between us human beings, the environment and the forces of nature. Away to the west it seemed to me that with straightened economic circumstances, nature has the upper hand. There were more derelict and abandoned properties along the roadsides and those that were still inhabited seemed to be finely balanced in terms of their future. Slowly but surely nature was reclaiming the earth. As we rode further east, the land took on a much more industrial feel with stock farming on a massive scale. Fewer dwellings, but more of them that looked well maintained. And in between the towns, clusters of small to medium sized buildings and facilities providing essential infrastructure for the industry. But everywhere I looked I was reminded that winning a living from the land here was not easy. Above all, I wished that I had the time and the talent to photograph and capture some of the scenes that I saw. This has surely already been done but I would have loved to record my own personal interpretations, ideally in black and white, to really record the bleakness of this place and the emotions I felt, in a way that my writings can only hint at.

There were two images that kept replaying in my mind. The first was an abandoned property, a very old, small house with outbuildings that were disintegrating. The roof of the house had fallen in. The adobe walls were crumbling. Trees and shrubs were sprouting through the floors. The yard was overgrown with wild grass tussocks and thorn bushes poking up through patches of sand and clay soil baked rock-hard by the sun. But the most remarkable sight was the old rusty cars and trucks that lay across the front yard. It was like looking at a graveyard of motoring history. I am no expert, but from what I could see the earliest cars probably dated from the 1930s and 40s. The most recent looked like they belonged in the 1980s and 1990s. The sense of humans fighting the forces of nature and loosing was very strong indeed. The second image was of those cattle waiting patiently to be slaughtered in the pens outside Dalhart. The human race here at the top of the food chain.

We made excellent progress and arrived at the first SAG well ahead of schedule. We had been anticipating this all morning as we had been promised the chance to get together with some hookers! Recognising a good business opportunity when they saw one, the Hookers had thrown open their doors to welcome us. The local Chamber of Commerce building where we had our comfort stop was all set to do some good business. And the 'madam' in charge of the establishment had the look of someone who had seen it and heard it all before. Now before you go getting the wrong idea readers, allow me to explain. We had reached the town of Hooker which was named after John (Hooker) Threikeld, who it is said, got his nickname from the Civil War General 'Fighting Joe' Hooker. Others say he was named after an old cattleman on the nearby Beaver River. Then there are those who assert that he was a skilled cattle roper – a hooker. But whatever the origin, there was no doubt about the provenance of the town. By all accounts, Hooker was a striking person, a big man with raven black hair and eyes, resembling, some say, an eagle. His features were enhanced by several gold teeth and his habit of wearing large diamond rings. Hooker died aged 92 in 1938 in Redondo Beach, California, which I rode through before the start of the tour. Today the town markets its name vigorously and all manner of Hooker memorabilia can be procured. I opted for a fridge magnet.

Leaving Hooker and the Hookers to their own devices we carried on east. Emil rode off into the distance to meet his wife Eve at the hotel. Pete and I continued onwards with Mary and together we crossed the state line out of Oklahoma and into Kansas. We made the obligatory stop for a photograph and then as we arrived at our destination in Liberal we engaged in a bit of sightseeing. The route sheet had noted that the Liberal Air Museum was worth visiting so that's exactly what we did. With over 100 aircraft spanning 90 years of aviation history on display, this was one of the country's largest air museums. Almost every type of aircraft was on display, from small home-built kit planes to relatively modern military jets. Liberal has a long association with aviation. It was a pilot training base during the Second World War and subsequently became a factory for the manufacture of light aircraft. As a little souvenir of our visit Mary bought me a sheet of paper with instructions on it for making it into a paper plane. She said she was very mindful of the weight restrictions on our luggage otherwise she might have got me something more substantial.

Having satisfied our appetites for aviation we agreed that it was time to satisfy our stomachs with some lunch. After signing in at our hotel we decided to eschew the more usual fare on offer from the run-of-the-mill chain eateries and headed back into Liberal in search of something more homely. Mary made some enquiries at a florists, as you do, and we then found ourselves at a small family-run Mexican establishment. Although from the outside it initially looked somewhat unprepossessing, once we had crossed the threshold we were warmly welcomed and our bikes were safely seated at their own table. Cold drinks were ordered and we were soon tucking into some tasty dishes. CV and I had a very nice shrimp burrito. Normally I am cautious about eating shellfish so far from the sea in a month without an 'R' in it. Although I am sure the shrimp had been frozen they were presented in a delicious sauce and wrapped in an extremely fresh and surprisingly light tortilla. Satisfaction indeed!

With time on our hands, Robin, who had been driving one of the support vehicles today, joined us and we went in search of Liberal's other main attraction, the Dorothy House. Yes, Liberal is The Land of Oz. So we walked on the Yellow Brick Road, watched out for Cowardly Lion, posed with the Tin Man and flirted – with other assorted characters. We all had a great deal of fun and for once it was nice to have some leisure time off the bike and mooch around. And guess who joined us later for dinner? Dorothy!

There was a rumour going around the dinner table in the evening that after leaving Liberal tomorrow there might be a bend or two in the road and even, just possibly, a junction! We'll also be heading through country to a city that has a lot of history. I can't wait!

Stage 18: Friday 1 June, Liberal to Dodge City (83 Miles)

After three days of riding on the 200-mile straight I was really hoping for a bit of variety today. A couple of bends ideally and, if I was really lucky, maybe even a turn at a junction. And as it transpired I had all three and then some. Today started with a heat haze and finished in a blur. The humidity had been building for the last couple of days and with the temperature rising again it seemed that I was in for another day in the sweaty saddle sauna.

Over the last few days I've probably written all I can for now about the landscape we've been riding through. The only thing I would like to add is that during the latter part of today's stage I almost felt I was at home in the Fens. Apart from the telegraph poles lining the roadside, the views were almost the same. A long straight two-lane road with intensively farmed fields growing arable crops including grain and maize but no sugar beet or oil seed rape as far as I could tell. Large irrigation gantries stretched across the fields, with farm buildings and grain driers protected by small copses and, from time to time even hints of hedgerows. The big difference is that the Fenland landscape is like a small-scale model version of this part of Kansas.

A defining feature of today was the Wildwest, cowboys and legendary lawmen, gangs, lawlessness and tough justice. Our first encounter was at the first SAG in the small town of Meade. And what a location – right next to the centre of the infamous Dalton Gang's hideout. During a relatively short career from 1890–92, the three Dalton brothers and their other associates carried out a number of train robberies in the area, helping themselves to significant sums of cash and other valuables. Their end came on 5 October 1892 when, in an attempt to outdo their rival Jesse James, they tried to rob two banks on either side of the same street on the same day. They were rumbled, partly due to the delaying tactics of a clerk in one of the banks. In the ensuing gunfight two of the brothers and two of their associates were killed. Another brother, Emmett Dalton survived despite receiving 23 gunshot wounds. Although he was sentenced to life imprisonment he was pardoned after 14 years. Today Meade is a rather quieter place and the Dalton's legacy lives on through a museum and several of the family's properties which have been preserved for posterity.

From Meade we made our way speedily and sweatily onwards with a quick pause to rehydrate in Minneola which is basically a crossroads with a gas station, a post office, some agricultural businesses and a few houses. The name, incidentally, derives from the names of the wives of the town's first settlers – Minnie Davis and Ola Watson. Then in a super-fast blast with a tailwind we arrived at the legendary Dodge City in seemingly no time. Founded in 1872 around the time that the railroad arrived, Dodge City has a fascinating history. As an important cattle town the drovers quickly left their mark on the town leading to it becoming known as the wildest town in the west. Famous lawmen including Wyatt Earp and Batt Masterton who, during his life, was also a professional gambler, journalist, army scout and an authority on prize fighting, were hired to bring law back onto the streets.

We received an excellent welcome on arrival at our hotel where bottles of ice-cold water and gift bags were handed out as we checked in. Closer inspection of my gift bag revealed the perfect accessory for tonight's dinner. Patience readers, all will be revealed – literally – in due course. After completing the usual end of ride routine involving the washing of my cycling kit and myself, Pete and I went in search of refreshment, specifically some beer. We arrived at a nearby bar and placed our order. The barkeep asked us if were going to pay cash or open a tab, adding that if we opted for a tab she didn't want to have to chase after us and beat the debt out of us. It seems that round here they still administer justice in the old-fashioned way! As it transpired we had a great time and were soon in conversation with several of the local worthies who were lining the bar. Yet again our British accents and our cycling activities were the ideal openers for a spot of parley with the local people. I have to say that they couldn't have been nicer and were genuinely interested in what we were doing. I could easily have spent a lot more time communing with them. Sadly, we had to leave – after paying our dues' in full of course, as we had to get ready for tonight's dinner at the intriguingly named 'I Don't Care Sports Bar'.

Now readers, I have a scoop for you. Included in the gift bag we received from the hotel was a red ladies garter. Dodge City still has a cancan show and the garter is symbolic of it. Mary and Robin hoodwinked me into believing that I was required to dress appropriately for the dinner so I hitched up the leg of my shorts and donned the garter. It was best described as a close fit! In a moment of madness while we were eating dinner and in the absence of any dancers, I took it upon myself to perform a little number for the team. I stood up on my chair, put one leg on the table and gave it my all. Before long the room was filled with the sounds of the team loudly singing Offenbach's 'Infernal Gallop', the tune for the cancan. Judging by the whoops, whistles, catcalls and even requests for 'more' it seems I may have inadvertently stumbled on to a new role in life. But what's a good ride and a hearty dinner without a little fun! I'm told that photographs are now available for sale on a website near you! Autograph anyone?

Stage 19: Saturday 2 June, Dodge City to Great Bend (87 Miles)

Today was notable for a number of reasons. First and foremost I won a bet and the grand sum of £1 and €1. All will be explained presently readers. Today's stage also proved to be the toughest stage of the tour so far. The route profile was gently downhill and at just over 80 miles looked pretty straightforward. What I hadn't anticipated was the wind, and what a sidewind it was! It never fell below 20 miles per hour for the whole stage. If that wasn't tough enough frequent gusts of up to 40 miles per hour during the morning more than made their presence felt, especially on the exposed sections of the stage.

Today was a day where my bike handling skills were fully tested. Riding in these conditions required considerable concentration, both to stay upright and also to avoid being blown into the rider next to me. Trucks approaching us created maelstroms which threatened to knock me off CV. Trucks overtaking us caused, if I was lucky, a sort of suction effect which pulled me along a tad faster for a few yards. If I was unlucky and the truck was unable to pull out then the effect was quite different – a rather violent vibration which rattled both me and CV.

Today The Fabs and Greg linked up with some other riders, Barry, Bruce and Cathy, to form a septet. Although we had ridden together intermittently on earlier stages, today was a case of seeking strength in numbers. We deployed a variety of tactics with mixed success. These included trying to form a through and off chain gang as well as a spot of echelon riding. With the combination of strong winds, lack of experience of riding together, variable road conditions and a mismatch of strengths it was hard work to maintain any consistency. I have an unfortunate tendency, when reaching the head of a chain gang to go hard which can put the riders behind me in difficulty leading to gaps opening and the loss of rhythm. This is largely the result of my solo riding on the windy, exposed flatlands of East Anglia where I tend to use headwinds as a surrogate for hills. Put me in a group in similar conditions and my poor etiquette usually provokes some acerbic comments from my companions! But, done well, riding in a disciplined chain-gang is almost an art form.

It was fascinating eavesdropping on the team over dinner. I think, that without exception, everyone had found this to be a hard day. But the chatter over the dinner table was the sound of weary contentment. Happy, weary contentment. I really enjoyed listening to riders sharing their perspectives and reflections. As I have said many times before, a good route makes a good ride; great riders make a great ride. As the tour progresses, days like today are the ones that build the relationships through shared experiences. What in my view is brilliant, is the amount of mutual support that is evolving as the tour progresses eastwards. There is little sense of competitiveness in the group. Instead we each have deeply personal experiences in our saddles and on our handlebars which we share, sometimes with a few words and sometimes with a few looks and nods across the dinner table. This is one of the things that makes me eager to get back in the saddle day after day.

The route continued to take us across the flatlands of Kansas on those now all too familiar long, straight roads often lined today by immense wind farms with their turbine sails rotating gracefully. Underneath was long green grass which swayed and rippled in the wind. Occasionally it almost seemed to be waving us along. At the small hamlet of Kinsley we reached a landmark, we had arrived exactly at the midpoint between San Francisco and New York. A very large billboard celebrated this point of geography. We were now literally at the middle of America. Following our own route from Los Angeles to Boston I estimated that we were about 400 miles short of our midpoint. But it was a very satisfying feeling to know that we were now officially in the centre of the US of A.

On most days we pass a National Historical Monument or Site. These are usually marked by a stone engraved with information about the site. Today, one such stone caught my eye. At Pawnee, just before reaching the town of Larned we passed the site of the birthplace of Farm Credit. The 280 acres of land here were collateral for a loan made in 1917 to a stockman to support his business. At that time loans were almost impossible to obtain or were very expensive (ten per cent interest per month was the base norm). As farming was vital to the US economy, Congress passed the Federal Loan Act which enabled long-term land loans to be made to farmers and ranchers. With start-up funding initially provided by Congress the mechanism has since repaid all the government money and is now entirely owned and self-financed by the farmers and ranchers it supports. These stone markers are a constant source of learning and enjoyment for me. This was another richly rewarding aspect of the tour and one that kept me fully engaged.

Our route sheet had highlighted the Pawnee Rock State Historic Site as a place worth visiting, even though it was slightly off the route. So a few of us did indeed divert and visit the site which is located on a small hillock, the only one for miles around. The hillock is capped by a viewing platform so, as CV has spent the last several days moaning about the lack of a good view, I decided to give her a treat. Access to the viewing platform was via a narrow steel spiral staircase which was no obstacle to us, despite several of my riding companions suggesting that we abandoned the quest. Abandon it? Not a chance! With perseverance and a bit of cursing we eventually managed to get to the top and CV was delighted with the view. I thought it was pretty good too.

Now, earlier I did say that today I won £1 and €1. Bruce, who was part of our group, had been dipping into my musings on my blog. He commented that I seemed to write quite a lot of stuff about history and so on and was pretty sure that I would tell the story of Pawnee Rock in today's report. Rather rashly, he even bet me £1 and €1 that it would appear on these pages. Well I had the last laugh as today's history lesson was the Farm Credit one. If you want to know about Pawnee Rock, which is actually a very interesting story, you will have to go on an Interweb safari. Bruce works in financial services so I think he appreciated the irony! And flexible gambler that I am, I told Bruce that instead of cash I would be happy to receive my winnings as a cold, golden, three to five per cent strength liquid poured out of a green or brown bottle.

Stage 20: Sunday 3 June, Great Bend to McPherson (64 Miles)

After yesterday's ordeal I was feeling more than a little apprehensive about what lay ahead today, as I am sure several other riders were. In the event we were worrying about nothing. A shorter route, sunny and warm but not overly hot air and, joy of joys, virtually no wind. And what wind there was was blowing from behind. We even had a start time half-an-hour later than usual – 8am which meant that I could complete my pre-ride routine at a much more leisurely pace. Within a few minutes of leaving, our group, which today included The Fabs (with Greg) as well as Bruce, Cathy, Mike and Robin, was spinning along effortlessly at around 20 mph. The change in our attitude was palpable. Instead of yesterday's grimaces and white knuckles there were lots of happy, smiling faces and even a fair bit of happy chatter and laughter. What a difference a day makes. Bliss!

We made such good progress that we reached the first SAG in Lyons, which Bruce told me was pronounced like the animal and not in the French way, in record time. CV had heard a rumour that some pumpkin pie would be on offer at the SAG and as we approached she sped up noticeably. Lyons is an attractive small town which has some nice tree-lined streets in the centre providing welcome shade. It is the county seat of Rice County and as we lounged around the SAG munching our pies a fine old building across the street caught my eye. Closer investigation revealed that this was the County Courthouse and the seat of the Honorable Richard E Burgess Jr., Magistrate Judge, Rice County. Seeing this, together with a chance remark from Robin over dinner later in the day, set me off on a train of thought. I wondered how a relatively small city, with a population of less than 4,000 people, justified a courthouse. The population of Rice County is about 10,000 people, McPherson was just 30 miles down the road and Great Bend 30 miles behind us. But I soon discovered that all was not what it seemed. Back home courthouses are usually concerned with the provision of justice whereas in the rural parts of the USA courthouses often also house a range of local and county government services. I was interested to discover the range of services available, not all of which were located within the courthouse building. In Rice, these included public health, economic development, planning, public works and the intriguingly named Noxious Weeds Department. I guess The Judge might keep a close watch on the goings on there. In the few minutes that I spent nosing around I also discovered that Rice is the second smallest incorporated city in Kansas. There was lots more to see but fearful that 'The Judge' might clap me in irons for loitering with intent in my lycra and as CV had polished off the last of the pumpkin pie, I decided it was time that we were on our way again.

The second half of the day's ride was pretty much like the first. Fast and relaxed. So fast that we arrived in McPherson around noon with time on our hands. As this was a Sunday most places in the older part of the town were closed. During a very brief sortie around the town I was amazed to discover that at one time it boasted an opera house. The preserved building is now both a film theatre and venue for hire.

I also spotted another courthouse and alongside it a statue of Major General James B McPherson, after whom the town is named. McPherson had a distinguished career and served in the Union Army during the Civil War. He lost his life at the Battle of Atlanta after being shot by Confederate soldiers. In a twist of irony, the leader of the Confederate forces here was his former classmate and childhood friend, Lt. General John Bell Hood. With some poignancy on hearing of McPherson's death, Bell wrote:

"I will record the death of my classmate and boyhood friend, General James B. McPherson, the announcement of which caused me sincere sorrow. Since we had graduated in 1853 and had each been ordered off on duty in different directions, it has not been our fortune to meet. Neither the years nor the difference of sentiment that had led us to range ourselves on opposite sides in the war had lessened my friendship; indeed the attachment formed in early youth was strengthened by my admiration and gratitude for his conduct toward our people in the vicinity of Vicksburg. His considerate and kind treatment of them stood in bright contrast to the course pursued by many Federal officers."

With most places closed and an early arrival at our hotel we adjourned to the nearby Freddy's Frozen Custard and

Steakburgers, a regional fast food outlet, to kill time. The place was absolutely heaving with, judging by their dress, families who had spent the morning at one of the many churches in town. The appearance of four sweaty, lycra-clad cyclists momentarily silenced the place and we were very definitely the centre of attention. With considerable aplomb we marched to the counter, placed our orders and claimed our seats acting throughout as if this was entirely normal behaviour, which it is – for us! Gradually, the assembled throng resumed its conversations though we continued to receive sideways glances from the patrons throughout our visit. Once we had feasted, we returned to the hotel, checked in, showered, changed into our 'street clothes' and went in search of a bar to guzzle some pre-dinner beer.

Chatting to Pete over a glass or three I happened to mention the challenge of finding enough sockets to plug my assorted inventory of electrical apparatus in to recharge. These included the Garmin, two bike lights, a digital camera, iPhone and iPad, electric toothbrush and CV's Shimanono Di2 gear. If I plug everything in at once, the lights in the room dim noticeably, such is the demand for electricity. A favourite place to find sockets is in the base of the lamp that sits on the nightstand. The problem I often encounter is that I connect up via a US/UK adaptor through a UK plug and a charger which means that depending on the location of the sockets on the lamp there is often not sufficient room to squeeze it in. "Don't you use the bible?" was Pete's response. "Use the bible?" said I. "Yes" said Pete, "I extract the bible from the nightstand and shove it under the lamp to raise it up high enough. I've even made a little game of it, trying to guess which drawer the bible will be in when I first come into my room." So dear readers, I'll end today's lesson by directing you to Genesis 1:3.

Stage 21: Monday 4 June, McPherson to Abilene (61 Miles)

Here's the story of today's ride in 65 words. We left McPherson and turned right and then immediately turned right again. Greg got on the front and we went very fast. After 22 miles we turned left and we went very, very fast. We stopped at the SAG in Durham and then started again. Then we went even faster than before. After 61 miles and 3 hours we arrived in Abilene and we stopped!

That pretty much sums up this morning's riding. With flat, fast roads, a tail wind and excellent co-operative riding, sharing out the work between us, we made excellent progress. In a few places we moved along effortlessly at around 30 mph. There was the hint of rain in the air (it didn't happen) which encouraged us to keep pushing on. But that's not the end of the story, Far from it. One of the things that kept me going was that I never know what I'm going to come across. Some days it was the countryside and the landscape. On other days it was the people that I encountered. Or perhaps, a piece of history – one of those historical markers. Today it was food. So readers, prepare your taste buds and whet your appetites.

Durham, where we had our SAG was an interesting, even quaint place and I had a very brief look around. Although in the 2010 census it had a population of only 112 people it is nevertheless classed as a city having been incorporated in 1906. The city takes its name from Durham cattle, a shorthorn breed, which originated in the north-east of England. In addition to the post office and a rather fine-looking Baptist Church one of the main attractions here is the Main Street Café which has been providing 'Good Ole Country Cooking' since 1995. The Café developed as a result of Wendell Wedel, the owner, who at the time was a welder, and as a contribution to a church auction he made an iron griddle to cook 600 hamburgers. Over time this led on to the development of a sausage-making enterprise, building on the work of his father who was a butcher. From there it was a relatively short step into starting up the café which is now known regionally and even nationally for the quality of its fare. The business has gone from strength to strength and its Friday night buffets are especially popular. Scratch the surface of an apparently sleepy town and it's surprising what you can find underneath.

While on this culinary theme I can tell you that we ended the ride in Abilene at the wonderfully named Joe Snuffy's old Fashioned Grill. And as it was lunch-time I had breakfast – eggs, over easy of course, bacon, sausage (Wendell's?), wheat toast and lashings of hot, flavoursome coffee. The origin of the name is quite amusing. The owner, Marty's dad, had the nickname 'Snuffy' after spending the change from a snuff buying errand on candy. Marty's dad got a spanking for his efforts and the nickname 'Snuffy' stayed with him thereafter. During his time in the army, Marty himself became known as Private Joe. So when he left to open the grill, Marty and his wife, Anja, decided to call it Joe Snuffy's. If you happen to be passing by don't hesitate to drop in. If the welcome we received was anything to go by you will not be disappointed. Just remember that it's closed on Tuesdays and Sundays.

5. A DAY IN THE LIFE

One of the things I really enjoy after each stage once CV and I have finished our post-ride ablutions is looking at our emails and the social media. As the tour progressed we found that we were receiving increasing attention with supportive emails, social media comments and likes, kudos and even a few comments on the Captain's Blog. It was a nice feeling to discover that lots of people were following our progress eastwards and urging us on. Quite a lot of people had questions for us but unfortunately the demands on our time meant we were usually unable to provide personalised replies. One of the most common questions we received was along the lines of "Can you tell me what a typical day on the tour is like?" Well in truth, each day had been quite different and there didn't seem to be a 'typical' day. But we thought it would be quite entertaining to try and describe our daily routine. So, get yourselves a beverage, sit down, and read and learn!

Our day usually starts at 5:45am when the cock crows. The cock is a very annoying ringtone on my phone. It has been totally effective and so far at least, has never failed to achieve its purpose. Quite often though I wake at about 5:15am and then spend the next half hour letting my mind reflect on the previous day's ride and on what lies ahead today. CV prefers to lollygag and has a rather more sedate approach to her morning power-up process. When I do finally swing my legs off the bed it all becomes a bit of a rush. The first thing I do, on the way to the bathroom, is to squeeze CVs tyres to check that they haven't gone soft overnight. If they have then she probably needs a tube change.

Once I'm in the bathroom I drink a couple of cups of cold water. Then after a quick wash and a scrub I don my lycra bib shorts, a t-shirt and some ordinary shorts. I prefer not to inflict the sight of my lycra-clad 'athletic' figure on my fellow hotel guests this early in the morning, especially those who aren't cyclists, as I'd like them to enjoy them breakfasts! A few years ago I was once asked to leave the breakfast room and not return until I was properly dressed!

Having dressed, it's time for the first critical event of the day, a visit to the ice machine to fill my Camelbak and water bottles, with the addition of a berry flavoured hydration tablet in the latter. I put the Camelbak and the bottles in my room fridge to keep them as cold as possible. Maintaining my hydration and electrolyte levels is absolutely essential to being able to sustain the intensity of riding day after day in the heat we've been experiencing.

When that's all completed I head down for breakfast around 6am. I usually have some fruit juice, a yoghurt and some cereal. Depending what else is on offer I may have some powdered scrambled egg and sausage (sliced, not links) or bacon. As the tour has progressed I've developed a bit of an aversion to the rather tasteless powdered scrambled egg and increasingly I have had some doubts about its nutritional value. So more often than not I have a toasted bagel or a couple of slices of brown toast. Sometimes there's a self-service waffle iron or pancake machine so I might ring the changes and have some with maple syrup. Other 'delicacies' on offer might include powdered egg omelette, usually with cheese and sometimes onions. The sight of cheese or onions at the breakfast counter usually sends me moving in the other direction! A few places have had 'proper' fresh fruit – melon, strawberries and blueberries, which if available I'll come back to for seconds and thirds, but never fourths! I'll wash everything down with a cup of coffee with fresh skimmed milk if it's available; black if it's not. UHT creamer and the Captain don't mix well at this hour. I've found the breakfasts quite challenging – I eat them mainly because I need the fuel and not because they have been especially appetising. In a few places when I suspected that the breakfast fare was likely to be underwhelming I went self-catering and bought some berries, nuts and seeds from a grocery the night before. CV is a lean, mean cycling machine so she rarely has breakfast.

Once breakfast is out of the way I head back to the bedroom to complete my ablutions and pack up my two kitbags. The tour organisers have imposed a weight restriction of 30 lbs of kit for the two bags we've been given. I've been pretty ruthless with what I've brought but even so space is tight, very tight. This means that each day I have a struggle to get my clobber stowed away and zip up the bags. I live in fear of one of the zips splitting, or worse. I've turned this process into a bit of a mind game too – and so far I haven't been beaten. I've had to resort to some cunning techniques though. For instance, I've got a pair of flip flops and a pair of trainers. The trainers have broad heels so I've discovered that the best approach is to mix and match by packing one trainer and one flip flop into each of the bags. It's these little details, readers, that I've discovered make all the difference. I live in constant fear of leaving some essential item behind. So far my count is two water bottles in the first week and, last week a complete set of riding kit, including my beloved spotty Bianchi jersey and some new and expensive bib shorts. The kit was in the closet in my bedroom in the hotel in Dalhart where I had hung it up to dry. I managed to phone the hotel once I realised my mistake and they had already retrieved it. I had hoped to be reunited with it in Abilene but it hasn't arrived yet so it could end up following me east across the USA for the rest of the tour!

Then it's time to don my riding kit, apply the various lotions I use (sun screen, lip salve for my nose and chamois cream). Then I have another look around the room to make sure I've haven't forgotten to pack anything. Once I'm fully kitted up I take my bags down to the hotel foyer to be loaded onto the support truck. Some riders bring their bikes down first and then return to collect their luggage. And some riders bring their bikes and their luggage down at the same time. Just saying readers. Just saying!

Once my bags are deposited outside the front of the hotel I then head back to my room to collect CV. At this point we usually have a little tête-à-tête to go over the day's route and the challenges that lie ahead. Over the years I've found that this can make a big difference to how my Bianchi family and I perform. As a relatively young thoroughbred CV is showing promising signs of responding well. As she gets more miles under her Michelins she is beginning to toss in a few helpful suggestions. Given that we are going to spend several intimate hours together each day it is vital to get any issues or wrinkles out into the open and then put them to bed before we depart along the tarmac. We have both agreed that communication between us is good, open, honest and non-judgemental. That isn't saying that we've always got it right. A couple of times CV has had to remind me, in the nicest way possible, to put my brain in gear before opening my mouth!

After our team meeting is complete we perform a daily ritual and tune out and spend a few minutes in quiet meditation and reflection. We are helped in this by our talisman Eduardo, a small, celeste painted stone that I balance on CV's saddle. Eduardo is named after Eduardo Bianchi our founding father and one of our inspirations. You can read more about him, Eduardo Bianchi not Eduardo Stone, in my book *Passione Celeste*. These few short minutes help CV and me to clear our minds ready for the adventure to come.

With a final look around the room to make sure that nothing has been left behind we are then ready to go public. We head down to the foyer, surrender our room key and chill out on the hotel forecourt. This is a good time to do two things. First, have a look around at the other riders to see how they're shaping up and, perhaps offer or even seek a few words of encouragement. Second, it's a chance to complete our final ride checks. These include another tyre pressure thumb test, powering up the Garmin and loading the day's route and switching on the rear flashing red light.

Next up is the morning route rap. Sometimes this feels like being back at school with the headteacher reading out a list of notices and dos and don'ts. Most of what we are told is well-covered in the daily route notes but it's a chance to highlight any particular hazards or features of concern. As the tour has progressed we have evolved into two start groups – an early group and a later group. The second group leaves about 30 minutes after the first. What's that I hear you saying? 'Slow' group and 'fast' group? I couldn't possibly comment!

At around 7:30am and with a cry of 'Andiamo' (look it up) I clip in and CV and I are underway. I like to start at the back of the group and watch the other riders head off. Unless I get caught at a traffic light this also means that I am unlikely to get lost straightaway. Once we're rolling I pick out the rest of The Fabs and within a mile or so we have usually formed up and are on our way on the day's stage.

After a few miles, apart from keeping half an eye on the road surface, gradients and so forth and half the other eye on The Fabs and any riders who are lurking in the vicinity, I normally travel to a parallel universe, cycling land, where I stay for most of the day. Time in cycling land is quality time. I do a lot of thinking here. You might be surprised what passes through the little grey cells. On a good day I even might transcend to quite a euphoric state. All through this another half an eye is taking in what we are passing through, the landscape, the history, the people I see. And if you're counting then you'll have worked out that I still have half an eye in reserve for emergencies or unexpected excitements. I might also chat to The Fabs. Sometimes if I am really lucky a train of events, a sighting or a random comment will trigger a thought that might ultimately form the basis for the day's blog story.

And then there's the singing! I like to sing when I am happy and I am happiest when I am riding. I usually 'sing' silently so that I don't disturb or frighten my fellow riders. Occasionally I might accidentally let rip which usually provokes a sharp response from anyone within earshot. If you've ever had the misfortune to be on the receiving end of my vocals you'll understand! What do I sing? Well everything and anything. I've even been known to try and teach CV some songs so we can duet.

By now some of you may be thinking that I have totally lost the plot. Well maybe I have but what I am really trying to say is that for me cycling on a good route with great riding companions is almost without compare. The soft hiss of rubber on tarmac, the near-silent whirr of chain over sprocket and the rush of the breeze through the vanes of my helmet and past my ears is what gets me up and riding day after day. And to be able to do this for several hours at a stretch. Well, I just feel so incredibly lucky.

Anyway, back to reality. Rather like the start of the day, the end is also pretty time constrained. Unless it's a short or especially fast stage we arrive at our destination by mid-afternoon. One of the great things about this tour is that when I arrive in my room my bags are already there and the air conditioning is on. I've dropped a few hints that a bottle of beer in an ice bucket wouldn't go amiss either but I'm not having any luck in that direction so far.

Once I'm in my room, I extract my bag of electrical leads and chargers and plug in the Garmin to recharge it. If necessary I will also locate the Bible to facilitate the charging process. God works in mysterious ways. Then I grab my sponge bag and dive under the shower fully clothed and just like professional racing cyclists I drown my lycra removing each item in turn and giving it a good soapy squeeze under the shower before rinsing it off. Once all the kit is off and thoroughly soaked I then wash myself. After towelling myself dry I'm out of the shower and, with a fresh towel, I roll up my bib shorts and walk on them to force out as much water as I can before hanging them up to dry. I repeat this for each item of clothing. This means that by the following morning my kit is dry and ready to be packed until it's next needed. And unless it's been a particularly hot and sweaty or a long day I find that with three sets of kit I can get by for a week before hitting the washing machine for a full-blown clean-up.

One of the things that I've noticed on this tour is that sometimes small, insignificant things can have a disproportionate impact and make me a bit irritable, or cranky as my American friends call it. Let me give you an example. Coat hangers. Yes, that's right. Coat hangers. Once I'm out of the shower and dressed, I grab a few coat hangers from the closet and use them to hang my damp kit on the shower curtain rail so that it can drip dry. In most hotels this is usually straightforward. Three coat hangers are all that I need. One for my bib shorts. One for my jersey. And one for my socks and mitts. Sorted! Well, in some hotels they use hookless hangers which attach to the hanging rail via a small clip with a hole in it. I have learnt that this is an attempt to thwart would-be coat hanger thieves. Really! Who steals coat hangers? When this happens I have to resort to folding the garments over the shower rail which usually means that they don't dry completely overnight and end up going into the kitbag slightly damp. Otherwise I hang the garments to dry on the hangers inside the closet, dripping on to the carpet below. Doing that was the reason why I left my spotty Bianchi jersey in Dalhart. There is one thing that's more frustrating than coat hangers with no hooks and that is coat hangers with hooks that are too small to hang on the shower rail. Don't get me started! Anyway, life is too short to get hung up on coat hangers, hahah! And whatever you do, do not mention Wi-Fi that doesn't work. We'll be here forever if you do!

With kit washing out of the way it's then time to attend to any minor issues with CV. I carry a pack of baby wipes with me so I can give her a quick facelift if needed. She loves to be pampered and sometimes purrs softly when I run the baby wipe back and forth over her crossbar. At the end of the stage immediately preceding a rest day, and before I have my shower, CV has the full spa treatment. A complete wash with soap, a chain de-grease, a frame polish and fresh chain lube.

Then we enjoy a bit of quiet time and review the day's events. If I'm really lucky an idea of what I might write about on my blog is already forming in my mind and I'll run it past CV. She's my fiercest critic. And if we've finished the stage early I might even fire up my iPad and start laying down some actual blog words. But more often than not that comes later. This is also when I upload my Strava data and then check in to see how my fellow riders, on the tour and back at home, have been getting on.

As the tour has progressed Pete and I have developed a pattern of seeking out a post-ride beer around 5pm. Sometimes this involves a bar but more often than not we head over to the nearest gas station to buy a few bottles and we set up a sort of open house back at the hotel when other riders come along and share a beer and commune with us. Judging by the growing numbers I think we are proving quite popular. I always enjoy listening to the other riders recount their day's adventures – especially from people who I haven't ridden with during the day.

Around about 6pm normally it's time for dinner which is either in the hotel, at a nearby restaurant or is catered in. We often eat in one of the chain restaurants such as Applebees or Crackerbarrel. There's nothing wrong with these places. As someone who enjoys his food, I find they can be a bit underwhelming. The chance to eat at an independent restaurant with ingredients that are locally sourced, prepared and cooked on the premises is an opportunity that I always seize. I wasn't expecting or seeking a gastronomic tour but night after night of the same sort of menu does wear me down a bit. And I guess that past tours in France, Italy and Spain have rather spoilt me! Leaving aside these minor grumbles about food, one of my tour satisfaction barometers is to listen to the level of chatter over the meal. And I can honestly report that most days the chatter level is both high and happy. That must say something.

By about 7:30pm most people are back in their rooms, as indeed am I. My first order of business is to extract tomorrow's cycling kit and get it ready. Then I make sure that anything I have unpacked, apart from today's kit which is still drying, is all in one place ready for tomorrow morning's zipper battle with the kitbags. Then it's my time. CV is all tucked up and quietly snoring in the corner of the bedroom – she needs at least 10 hours beauty sleep. I get my iPad out, power it up, close my eyes and clear my mind for a minute before I start typing and see where it leads me. By 10pm I have usually finished and filed the day's story and also done all my social media stuff. Then in the words of Zebedee from the Magic Roundabout it's "Time for bed".

So there you have it. A day in the riding life of Captain Century and CV. I hope I've answered many of your questions. CV and I will start all over again tomorrow. Please join us for 7:30am. Don't be late! See you on the start line.

ABILENE TO CHAMPAIGN : 7 DAYS, 623 MILES

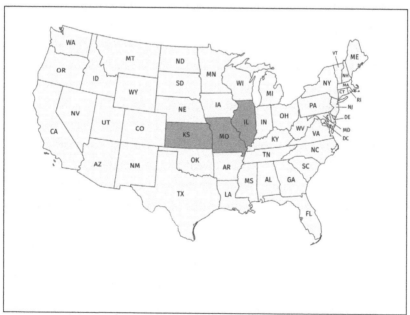

6. ONWARDS, ALWAYS ONWARDS

Rest Day: Tuesday 5 June, Abilene

Abilene, the location for our third rest day, boasts a number of diverse attractions including the Greyhound Hall of Fame and the Seelye Museum of which more in a while. The city is probably most famous as the place where Dwight Eisenhower, general and then president, lived from the age of two and which he considered as his home. His life is commemorated in the presidential Library and Museum which is one of the main attractions in the town. The Presidential Libraries are a network of 13 institutions which are administered under the umbrella of the National Archives and Records Administration. They house the papers, records and other historical materials of every president from Herbert Hoover (31st President, 1929–1933) to George W. Bush (43rd President, 2001–2009) and are open to the public. Exhibitions about the presidencies are also displayed. The records of other presidents are also available but independently managed. At the time of writing, work on the Barack Obama Centre, in Chicago, is about to begin with opening scheduled for the early 2020s. During our visit the Eisenhower Museum was closed and undergoing a major renovation with some of the exhibits on temporary display in the adjacent library. Speaking at the library's inception in 1959, Eisenhower said:

> "When this library is filled with documents, and scholars come here to probe into some of the facts of the past half century, I hope that they, as we today, are concerned

primarily with the ideals, principles, and trends that provide guides to a free, rich, peaceful future in which all peoples can achieve ever-rising levels of human well-being."

That seemed like a fine sentiment to me.

With no shortage of potential entertainment on our rest day Pete and Robin went for a 50-mile ride in the morning! Mary and I opted for a more leisurely approach and rode the one mile into the city centre and enjoyed a lazy morning chatting over coffee in the rather excellent Amanda's Bakery and Bistro. It was a nice feeling to simply chill out and forget about the relentless pedalling east consuming the mileage that had dominated the last week. Don't misunderstand me. The riding was great and I was looking forward to starting the next phase tomorrow. But sometimes it's just nice to stop the conveyor belt and take stock. Amanda's was just the place to do that. After a couple of hours of not doing very much Robin and Pete joined us, glowing and hungry from their ride so we lingered a bit longer for some lunch. I had spied an old sign on the bakery wall about an ice cream parlour which I discovered had been relocated to the drug store next door. I just had to go and investigate. And I was not disappointed. A wide variety of ice creams were on offer and the range of toppings and 'extras' defied description. I settled for a modest cone with some salted caramel.

Having refuelled and recharged our batteries and with an hour or so to spare we decided to do a little bit of sightseeing. Our chosen sight was the Seelye Mansion which was just a short ride away from the bakery. As is sometimes the case, not everything is what it seems. Our first clue came when we arrived and checked in at reception. We were greeted by another rider, Ichiro who looked rather shell-shocked. He seemed lost for words and when he saw his bike his face lit up and he jumped on it and pedalled away faster than any of us had ever seen him do. At the time we thought his speechlessness was the result of the splendours he had seen and his speedy departure reflected a need to explore more of Abilene's touristic attractions in the remaining time available. Little did we know.

Built in 1905 for Dr and Mrs Seelye at a cost of $55,000 the mansion has been described as one of the finest historic homes in Kansas. With 11 bedrooms, a ballroom, a dining room, a music room, a library and a bowling alley the mansion is richly furnished including an elegant grand piano and gold furniture. Every room houses a treasure trove of historical artefacts giving an unusual insight into the lives of the original owners and their successors. The Seelye's made their fortune in medicine from the 1890s with their products and 'cures' sold by travelling salesmen in the neighbouring states and beyond. Whether or not the products, many of which were patented, had any real medicinal value has been the subject of much debate.

All very well you might say. Where's the catch? Well, what we had hoped would be a reasonably fast-paced tour turned out to be anything but. Our guide, the present owner seemed determined to share the details and history of every item on display including each of the original Edison designed electrical fittings, light switches, bulbs and so forth. Our host's enthusiasm was unlimited but unfortunately it went far beyond what we, as casual visitors could cope with. Robin saved the day for us and in her best Californian manner explained to our host that we were on a very tight deadline and had to leave. Although he looked somewhat disappointed at our abrupt departure a hint that we might one day return brought a smile back to his lips. As we hastened out the front door we now understood Ichiro's shell-shocked expression! When we saw him later we learnt that he had been inside for several hours!

Stage 22: Wednesday 6 June, Abilene to Topeka (108 Miles)

After our restful rest day which we spent resting we were ready to get back on the road and continue eastwards across Kansas and beyond. Little did I know before setting off what delights lay in store today on the road ahead. Several years ago a colleague of mine, a mentor and a person who I had huge respect for, told me that when I was writing or giving a talk I should always start with my conclusion. So here you are readers, I'm going to quote a few words from Lou Reed which exactly captured how I felt by the end of the day: "Oh, it's such a perfect day." Lou's soaring vocals, the strings and the simple piano riff perfectly summed up what CV and I were feeling. You should listen to the song. It's on his Transformer album, released in 1972. And while you've got the album playing the fifth song, 'Walk On The Wild Side' is pretty good too. I do like to cross over to the wild side from time to time. I'm streaming the album as I am writing this account of the day's ride. I am sorry if I've gone a bit sentimental here but rides on days like this are truly magical.

So what was it about today's stage that made me feel like this? After the last super-fast stage, today we had decided to be tourists and ride at a rather more sedate pace. I spent quite a lot of the stage riding with Robin. Although we rode together, much of the time we did this in silence with each of us soaking up the experience and the atmospherics of the scenery we passed through. Although the weather was very hot and humid this was more than compensated for by the delightfully small, quiet and mostly traffic-free country roads we travelled along. The countryside now was much greener and there were more trees, hedges, copses and woods. The terrain was gently undulating and the roads picked their way through the landscape seeking out interesting and stimulating routes. Single houses and small villages appeared along the way proving no shortage of eye candy. And some of it was entirely unexpected. At one place we passed a long fence with wooden animals and nursery rhyme characters carved into it. At another, the call of a peacock enticed us to make a small diversion to try and spot it (we did!). And at another place Robin and I swept round a bend in the road to be greeted by the most magnificent view of the road sweeping down in front of us through a deep, tight rocky gorge. The view literally took our breath away. The incredibly smooth surfaces of what seemed to be minor county roads were a delight to ride on, accompanied by the soft swish of rubber on tarmac as the soundtrack to our progress.

The intense heat and humidity meant that this was one sweaty ride so we drank litres and litres of water and the SAG stops were critical to ensure we could take on fresh supplies. At our first stop in White City, after about 35 miles, we were joined by a local man who, when he discovered what we were doing, insisted on receiving advance details of next year's tour so that he could ensure the city, founded in 1871 and today with a population of 600, laid on a civic reception! More often than not I found that the people in the small rural communities we passed through were really interested in what we were doing and were more than happy to chat or answer our questions.

Even though we had refilled our bottles at the first SAG it wasn't long before we needed a cold drink. The small city of Alta Vista, which was about one mile off our route, looked the most likely place to find a store or a gas station. Robin and I decided to make the detour down Main Street to see what we could find, encouraged by my observation that there was another road out of the city that we could use as a shortcut back to the route. Arriving in the city centre we found the Barnyard Café which provided us with ice cold sodas and bottled water. Perfect! With our thirsts quenched we set off to rejoin the route. "Follow me," was my call to Robin, "I can see on my Garmin exactly where we need to go." Well I had spoken too soon because what my Garmin didn't show was that 'the road' was unsurfaced. More like a trail than a road. Risking the, hopefully, small possibility of a puncture, we carried on regardless. We could see the stony, dirt covered track stretching ahead of us for about a mile to the point where it reached the tarmac and our official route. Suddenly, there was the most ferocious barking and a huge, wild-looking dog came bounding out of a driveway towards us. Without a moment's hesitation Robin stamped on her pedals and in a puff of dust was away from the irate hound in a jiffy. I adopted a more hesitant, and probably less chivalrous approach by braking and trying to stare down the irate canine. Ever since I was ravaged by a rabid Alsatian as a kid I have had a longstanding fear of large, barking dogs that bound out of driveways. This dog stood totally still returning my hesitant gaze with an unblinking stare. I think I read somewhere that trying to stare down an angry dog invites more trouble. Eventually, I summoned the courage to move forward and passed by the dog who continued to stand guard on its threshold. When I eventually caught up with Robin she said, in a rather matter of fact tone, that I would only ever have been at risk if I had tried to ride down the driveway. I suspect she thought I was a bit of a wimp!

The route notes and the stage briefing this morning both flagged up a special treat for today. Pies. And not just any pies but award-winning pies. The Somerset Hall Café by the crossroads in Dover has achieved a national reputation having won several awards over many years. It first achieved national recognition ten years ago in 2008 when Norma Grubb the café's pie-maker, won the Best Pie in America award. This success transformed the café and the town of Dover. People came from near and far to sample the pies and others wrote in asking for pies by mail order. It is estimated that Norma made more than 10,000 pies by the time she retired at the age of 89. Norma passed away in 2011 leaving 23 grandchildren, 29 great grandchildren and 11 great-great grandchildren.

The café occupies a large open space in a building that dates from 1868. When we arrived a glass display cabinet hinted at what was on offer. At the back were bags of flour waiting piled high, ready for the next pie making session. Old farming posters and artefacts lined the walls. Formica tables were set out ready for customers. The place was popular, very popular, with a constant stream of local people, farm workers and their families I guess, dropping in for lunch. Service was swift and while we were waiting large glasses were filled with ice cold water to help cool us down. And what of the pies? Well, being a bit of a traditionalist I had a slice of apple pie and vanilla ice cream and it was good. But if the truth has to be told, Mary's Pecan Fudge Pie was simply divine. I offered to swap half of my apple pie for half of hers, but she wasn't having any of that! I didn't even get a photograph of it, but she did tease me with a couple of tastes!

Riding into Topeka after eating the pies was almost an anti-climax. As we neared our destination in yet another out of town area development it struck me that maybe, just maybe there were some elves driving ahead of us to unpack and construct the rather anonymous and featureless, but totally functional and convenient suburbs that our hotels are located in. Then when we leave tomorrow morning the elves will magically appear, take everything down and rush it over to our next stage town. Only kidding!

Once I had checked in to the hotel and showered I had a swim in the hotel's pool to loosen up before dinner. And the just perfect day ended with, for once, a tasty meal; a nice light and wholesome shrimp stir fry. Crispy vegetables, some soft succulent shrimp, with hints of chilli, garlic, honey and ginger on a bed of brown rice. I couldn't have asked for better than that. Chatting to Pete over the meal, he remarked that he could easily have kept going for another 20 miles, so much was he enjoying himself. Of course he does go for rides on rest days! And do you know what readers? There was a rumour circulating that tomorrow was going to be at least as good. I do hope it's true! Just a perfect day!

Stage 23: Thursday 7 June, Topeka to St Joseph (85 Miles)

Unfortunately today's stage didn't quite live up to my expectations. Having enjoyed some outstanding riding on quiet minor roads yesterday I was hoping for more of the same today. Instead we found ourselves on some bigger roads with shoulders and rather more traffic, including a few drivers who were up there with the worst on the tour so far – honking their horns and passing us with the minimum distance. We also had a bit of cloud cover, a lightish headwind but thankfully the humidity wasn't quite as fierce as yesterday. For me the best parts of the stage were the first few miles and the last few miles. In between, well Pete summed it up nicely: "There's not a lot to photograph!"

Our route out of Topeka was quite interesting. Basically we left pre-fab hotel land in the capable hands off the elves and rode into, and then across, the heart of the city along some lovely leafy roads and past a nice assortment of residential architecture. The roads were quite busy until we reached the centre of the city when we started riding against the flow of traffic with people going to work. As we arrived in Topeka yesterday, Pete and I had been on the lookout of for our customary photo stop with the city limits sign but didn't see one. So I was delighted, when paused at a traffic light, to feel a nudge from CV who nodded towards a rather fine sign straddling the road. The lights were red so I was able to grab a shot for the collection. Pete cheated and downloaded one from the Interweb at the end of the day!

We carried on across Topeka and through the suburbs until we reached State Route 4 which we then rode along for the next 30 miles, passing through the first SAG along the way. I had a spot of fun before this as I pulled over for a brief chat with Robin and Mary who were on support duties today in one of the SAG vehicles, leaving Pete and Emil to head off up a gentle climb and over the horizon. I then set off in pursuit and once I had reached the top of the incline I got onto the drop bars, wound it up through the gears and went full gas for about 3 miles, eventually catching Pete and Emil shortly before the SAG. Then another 25 miles took us to the next SAG and a cooling milkshake at a Dairy Queen.

From there it was a short hop, skip and jump to Atchison and the muddy Missouri River to say 'Goodbye Kansas' which has been our home over the last six days. A couple of signs caught my eye. The bridge across the Missouri was named after Amelia Earhart, the aviator, who I subsequently discovered was born in Atchison in 1897. The house she was born in was built in 1861 in a Gothic Revival style (work that one out for yourself) and is now preserved as a historic building with a museum.

The other sign that caught my eye was a reference to Lewis and Clark and a nearby State Park named after them. This set me thinking. I was aware of them and their explorations, but I didn't know much more. With a spot of Giggling on the Interweb later that day I am now much better informed. Their pioneering expedition between 1804 and 1806 was focussed very much on exploring, understanding and documenting the territories of western America for the purposes of trade and sovereignty. What really surprised me when I started reading about their expedition was how relatively recently their work has been properly recognised in contemporary historical writings. One hundred years after their travels many of their achievements were reported at a fairly superficial level. A complete set of their diaries was only published in 2004 to celebrate the bicentennial of their explorations. I've made a note to do some more reading after the tour is finished.

Almost as soon as we had crossed the state line into Missouri, the Show Me State, the road surface took a turn for the worse. Rough tarmac and potholes made me feel that I had suddenly been transported back to Britain! For the next 10 miles we ground our way along until after a quick stop for a cold drink, we arrived at the outskirts of St. Joseph. From there we rode along the South West Parkway which was a delight. A lovely smooth surface, which with a few switchbacks and rolling hills amongst lots of trees in an evidently affluent landscape was pure pleasure to ride. This struck me as the perfect place for criterium racing. If only! Even the minor inconvenience of a front wheel puncture made little difference to how I felt. In five minutes with some help from Emil and Pete I was rolling again. Eventually we reached the outskirts of 'modern' St Joseph and our hotel. And guess what? Those darned elves had arrived there before us again!

Sitting in the foyer of the hotel waiting to chat to other riders as they rolled in, I noticed Mary enter the hotel looking quite upset. Catching my eye, she walked over, sat down and I could see that she was really troubled by something. Eventually she looked at me, with a tear in her eye, and simply said, "Robin's been sacked". I was speechless. Ever the professional, and mindful of the client-staff relationship, Mary understandably didn't want to share any more details. As far as I could tell there had been some sort of disagreement between Robin and the tour company owners. Robin and Mary had formed a close friendship, each supporting the other, and I could see that Mary was feeling quite isolated and alone. Over the last few days, and especially since our rest day in Abilene, Pete, Robin, Mary and I had become good friends. Only 24 hours ago Robin and I had shared and enjoyed a wonderful day riding together. Robin was now the third member of the tour crew to fall by the roadside. At this rate there would be no one left to support us by the time we reached Boston. Not what I had expected or anticipated when I had chosen to ride with CrossRoads. It really did seem that the riders would have to look to each other at a new level for mutual support. I told Mary that I would be very happy to help her in any way I could, and I urged her to keep one eye looking over her shoulder in case of the unexpected.

Stage 24: Friday 8 June, St. Joseph to Chillicothe (87 Miles)

At the morning route briefing there was no mention of Robin's departure. It was as if she had never existed. Another white washing. I was tempted to ask some pointed questions but, rightly or wrongly I decided to keep my own counsel, at least until I knew a bit more. Several other riders shared my perspective and together we resolved to work collectively to try and overcome any weaknesses in the tour support. It was with more than a touch of sadness and quite a lot of concern that we rolled out of the hotel forecourt on the day's stage.

If yesterday's riding was a little disappointing, today at least it was much more rewarding. Sunny skies, albeit in very humid conditions and a route that was mostly on quiet roads rolling through lush green countryside was precisely the recipe for an enjoyable day's riding. 'Rolling' was probably the word that best captured the essence of the day – a succession of short and usually not too steep climbs and descents. I say 'usually' because every once in a while a sharp little ascent would creep up on me and give my leg muscles an extra workout.

The critical factor in riding these rolling climbs is to select the right gear ratio at the right time. Use too high a gear for too long and it gets tough and changing down to a lower gear under load gets risky with the possibility of shipping the chain or worse still breaking it. I've never had the misfortune to personally suffer a chain break in this situation though I have seen it happen to other riders. Shipping or breaking the chain, the end result is usually the same; the ignominy of falling off and ending up on the tarmac often in front of other riders.

Choose too low a gear too soon and you lose the advantage of any momentum gained on the preceding descent. It sounds easy but based on my experience today it is not. Climbs which look gentle from afar hold many surprises – a steeper or longer than expected gradient and perhaps worst of all, a false summit. Get it right and it's really rewarding riding. Get it wrong and it can be both demoralising, especially on a long stage, or strength sapping on a hot humid day like today. I reckon I did OK today with, I estimate, an 80 per cent success rate.

I also spent some time today riding on my own and I enjoyed the chance to immerse myself in my own quiet reflections and thoughts. Reflections on the tour so far and thoughts of the people, new friends and 'cousins' that I have ridden with, including those who have now left the tour. Riders who have left us as they always intended to and members of the tour support crew who, in explicably, seem to be falling by the wayside as the tour progresses eastwards. I found this troubling because the original CrossRoads offer that I signed up too promised a good level of support on the road. Drawing on my own experience as a qualified tour leader, the tour was starting to feel quite exposed on the support front.

As I am fond of saying, good routes make good tours and this is a good tour, but it's some of the people who I ride with who transform a good tour into a great tour. So to my riding companions, past and present I say, in the time-honoured cycling way "Chapeau". You all know who you are from our conversations, and the great company I have enjoyed and shared with you on the road thus far. Having concluded my mid-stage reflections I turned my mind back to the route and the countryside we were passing through.

Our route took us mostly in an easterly direction and with the benefit of a light tailwind it was fairly easy going, climbs excepted. Our first SAG was at Maysville where we were accosted by a hack from the local paper who wanted to get a scoop on our tour for the *DeKalb County Record-Herald*. A small group of us lined up for a photocall outside the gas station. There was a stack of copies of the latest edition, published the previous day, on the counter of the gas station shop. A cursory glance suggested the paper was an important source of local news and information – the lead article was a report on the monthly meeting of the Osborn R-O School District. As far as I can ascertain, the paper is only published in print form, bucking the trend back home in Britain to move increasingly towards Interweb publication. As I moved off I wondered if we would make next week's edition. Front page news?

From Maysville we continued along the rolling roads until we joined a particularly rough, busy and unpleasant stretch of State Route 6 for around 15 miles. Once we turned off this we were back on much quieter roads, again with the rollers. A succession of long, straight transects meant that there were some spectacular views of the route ahead which often looked like a ribbon had been laid down stretching into the distance several miles ahead. The green and well-treed landscapes with, increasingly, fields of maize in between the delightful farmhouses made for exhilarating viewing.

Gradually, as we closed on our destination the density of properties increased and at around 85 miles we turned onto

State Route 66 after pausing to take the customary end of stage town-sign photo. As we turned onto the main road I looked back over my shoulder. It almost felt like I was exiting through some gates and leaving a magical world behind me. The last few miles had been especially enjoyable. Tough riding yes, on some of the steepest climbs of the day. But rewarding riding too; very rewarding.

Chillicothe, and there was some debate in the peloton as to the correct pronunciation of the name, is derived from the Shawnee language – meaning Big Town referring to a settlement about a mile from the present-day city. Chillicothe's claim to fame is that it is the 'Home of Sliced Bread'. In 1928 the Chillicothe Baking Company began selling pre-sliced bread through local grocers – apparently the first time that pre-sliced bread was sold commercially in the world. As if to reinforce this I smiled as I passed a grocery store – the Sliced Bread Market. Now there's a thing!

In a break from our usual end of stage routine, Pete and I got haircuts once we had showered and changed. For $12 and an interesting chat with folk in the barber shop I got a nice neat number 3 which should set me up for the rest of the tour. Thus far there hasn't been much discussion about politics with the people I've met along the way. Well, today in what was I sensed a Republican stronghold, that changed when the barber asked me for my thoughts on the President, Mr Permatan. When someone working close to your skull with a sharp implement asks a question like that, careful answers are needed. Very careful answers. I think I muttered something along the lines of "he certainly seems to be very visible". Whatever it was I said was fine because I wasn't attacked and my haircut was completed to my satisfaction. And before you get the wrong idea, the reference to 'Mr Permatan' is my tag. And I certainly did not offer that to the head cutter!

Stage 25: Saturday 9 June, Chillicothe to Kirksville (75 Miles)

Today's report picks up where yesterday's finished – rollers, lots of rollers. The consensus over breakfast was that there 148 rollers to be traversed. Who counts these things? We rolled out of Chillicothe along US-36 E heading for Brookfield, 36 miles away. Above us, grey clouds and heavy air suggested a change in the weather might be on the way. The air even felt wet, if you can imagine that. Ahead of us lay an angry yellow sky with sunbeams and showers falling on the horizon. Amazingly we haven't had any rain on the road since we left Los Angeles nearly one month ago. I'm going to repeat that loudly for the benefit of my British cycling chums. WE HAVEN'T HAD ANY RAIN FOR NEARLY A MONTH! Looking at the daily weather forecasts we seem to have had the most extraordinary luck as our route has meandered eastwards around some pretty severe weather, including a few tornadoes.

As we rode along on a quiet early Saturday morning I found myself thinking of a song by The Doors – 'Riders on the Storm' from their iconic album, L.A. Woman. It opens with the sound of rain falling and after a few seconds John Densmore and Robby Krieger lay down a rolling pattern on percussion and guitar before Ray Manzarek comes in on electric piano with a melody that sets the pattern for the song. After about 45 seconds Jim Morrison joins in with the simplest of lyrics delivered in his languid style. The song is hugely atmospheric and over the next 7 minutes it grows and builds to a fabulous conclusion. If you haven't heard it, then give it a listen. It properly captured what I was feeling this morning on US-36 E. Once again today we were really lucky and the stormy weather dissipated leaving blue skies, hot sun and that strength sapping humidity. It seems as if Zeus, the god of clouds, rain, thunder and lightning is keeping a distance from us – for now at least!

A couple of miles before we left the highway I had the misfortune to suffer a rear wheel puncture, my first for several days, the cause being another of those tiny truck tyre wires. With help from Pete I was soon up and running again (we've had a lot of practice) and we turned off at Brookfield for a water refill stop, a sort of halfway house SAG. From here we were onto the roller coaster road. Always up or down and rarely level.

A combination of gradients which varied between two and ten per cent, the hot sun and high humidity slowly sucked the energy out of my legs. I also realised that I was drinking significantly more water and electrolyte energy drink than I normally do. And I was sweating buckets – my jersey and base layer were drenched. On the positive side, the landscape was outstanding. The rolling terrain, a mix of open fields – arable and grazing, trees, hedgerows and woods meant that there was a lot to look at and take in. I passed countless delightful properties – farms and ranches as well as houses, many of which were tucked away in the woods. They all gave the appearance of an extremely well-managed countryside. Add to this the quiet, well surfaced roads and once again this was another day of excellent, if challenging riding.

Pete had a minor mechanical when his drivetrain appeared to be slipping which made gear changes to cope with the gradients very difficult. Initially the cause seemed to be rear wheel axle bolt which was loose. Closer inspection at the end of the stage suggested a faulty freewheel hub so he will need to get it looked at on our next rest day in a couple of days. In the meantime he's managed to implement a workaround so he's good to go.

Riding along, it dawned on me that this would be a great route for a road race, or better still, a stage on a multi-day tour. I imagined a small group going up the road and quickly gaining a few minutes once they were out of sight of the peloton which would coast along behind them. Perhaps even a couple of daredevil breaks for glory from the lead group. Would they reach the finishing line before being swept up by the peloton with a sprint finish to decide the result? I could see a few motorcycles with TV cameras and a helicopter or two hovering above. I am sure this would make for exciting viewing. Normally, I find watching live road racing a tad dull and prefer to catch up with the edited highlights. Today's road seemed to me to have loads of potential to showcase some fast, furious and exciting professional racing. I wonder where I've put Christian Prudhomme's phone number? For non-cycling readers he's the head honcho of the Tour de France or La Grande Boucle which, incidentally, is almost upon us. Will the Froomedog complete his quintet of victories to join the greats?

Like most of the riders, by the time I reached the SAG at 50 miles I felt rather flat. Some fresh fruit salad helped to lift my spirits somewhat. It's surprising how little things like this can be a real morale boost. As I chowed down my apple, grapes, melon and orange I sensed that everyone around me was feeling pretty drained. The heat and humidity coupled with the relentless climbs on the road seemed to have sucked the life out of my fellow riders. Normally we are a fairly lively bunch, keen to share our insights on the day so far – especially with riders we don't see often. There is usually a lot of happy chatter. Today it was a lot quieter. John, who I quite often catch up with at SAGs, observed that it was 25 miles to the finish. Then, and quick as a flash, he persuaded Mary to stream the Edwin Starr song on her phone. Do you know it? It opens with some bold and funky sax playing backed by the beat of bass and drums with Edwin's raw and powerful vocals driving the song forward with a pulsating rhythm. There's a great YouTube video of Edwin performing the song at his last ever concert in Stuttgart in 2003 which is well worth seeking out. The whole band are giving it everything and are 'marching' relentlessly forward on the stage.

In a bold effort to lift the spirits of my flagging colleagues I resorted to my tried and trusted approach. With the song pulsating from Mary's phone my legs started twitching and I was quickly up on the picnic table giving it large in full boogie mode. Well, I like to feel that I caught the moment but maybe the smiles and the laughter of my fellow riders were just a polite response to yet another of the Captain's eccentricities. I've been told that there's a video of my movements somewhere on the Interweb. And no, I am not going to tell you how to find it. If you really are that keen to see 'the performance' you can do the searching yourself.

Anyway, it did the trick for me and I completed the last 25 miles without too much of a struggle. I was really glad to reach the hotel in Kirksville and although this had been a tough day, after a shower and a swim it was also a very satisfying one. I reflected on a job well done and the 148 rollers conquered. Or was it 149? Or maybe 147?

Stage 26: Sunday 10 June, Kirksville to Quincy (75 Miles)

This morning we had some very sad news. One of the tour team, Mike, unfortunately had a serious accident yesterday and was airlifted to hospital. While the full details were still unclear it appears that he collapsed and crashed while going downhill resulting in a head injury. I was able to ascertain that he is being looked after in hospital and that his family were with him. As you can imagine, the mood today was rather subdued. Mike was one of the older riders on the tour and although I hardly knew him I was constantly impressed at his ability to keep going under all circumstances. He came across, to me at least, as quite a private person, comfortable in his own company and happy to ride solo. Whenever I passed him on the road I always said hello and invariably received a nod and a smile back. A couple of days ago he had sat with me at breakfast and unusually for him started a conversation by telling me that he had been reading my blog and he thought that I might be interested in the writings of another cycling tourist in the USA and Europe. I gave him my email address and later that day he sent me a message with some links to the rider concerned. So like all of the other riders I started the day with a heavy heart and I dedicated my day's efforts to him and his family. Throughout the day Mike was with us in spirit as my fellow riders extended their thoughts, prayers and their good wishes to Mike and his family at this difficult time.

After yesterday's tough stage on the rollers in the heat and humidity, today was something of a transition stage. By common consensus, and with another century stage tomorrow, we had decided to rein it in a bit and ride easy. The 'we' here comprised The Fabs (Pete, Emil and me) with the addition of a couple of guest artistes in the shape of Cathy (aka Person Number Three) who comes from San Francisco, and Bruce who hails from Nashville. We set the tempo and tapped out a good rhythm on the tarmac. At school assembly this morning three milestones for the day were highlighted and I will tell you about them presently.

At this point I should explain that Cathy acquired her 'Person Number Three' nickname a few stages ago. We had all arrived at our hotel to discover that the Wi-Fi network was down. Now there is one thing that is guaranteed to make cyclists cranky and that's a faulty Wi-Fi connection. We all have data that we're anxious to immediately upload to our Strava accounts. And then there are emails, social media and so forth which all need to be accessed. Immediately! So, a group of frustrated cyclists gathered in the foyer with one of the hotel staff who was clearly feeling the burden of responsibility and struggling to find a solution. After about 15 minutes, a mild enquiry from Cathy about progress towards a solution was met with said employee looking round our group and then looking Cathy straight in the eye, saying "Wait your turn Person Number Three". From there on Cathy was always going to be Person Number Three, to me at least. And to Cathy's credit she saw the funny side!

Most of the day was spent on quiet roads, quieter than usual because today was Sunday. Despite our plan to hold back and ride easy, we found ourselves making excellent progress, aided by a light tailwind. Along the way we passed over the intriguingly named Troublesome Creek and I stopped to get the requisite photograph. The name is a reference to the frequent flash floods that occur in the area. The scenery for much of today's stage wasn't that special – mostly unremarkable or underwhelming rather than unattractive, and lacking yesterday's splendour. An early highlight was being passed by an Amish man driving a horse and cart. We exchanged friendly greetings as we passed by each other. I had heard that as we progressed eastwards we would see more Amish people and I was looking forward to this and seeing their villages and farms. In the era of fast living and high technology, I was keen to observe a little more of their traditionalist approach to life, even if from afar.

Our first milestone coincided approximately with the SAG. We had now completed 2,000 miles on our journey from Los Angeles. There were 'only' 1,400 miles to go and there was a clamour to get the necessary photos for the scrapbook. It seemed like an eon ago that we left Manhattan Beach to embark on the tour. So much has happened since we left – lots of scenery, lots of sweat, and lots of satisfaction. For me though, the most precious parts of the tour were the friendships and the sense of a shared objective, a common purpose, that brought us together, and even, sometimes, a shared struggle to complete each stage. There seemed to be a bond developing between us that I hoped would carry us all the way to Boston and beyond. With the loss of most of the support crew, riders were relying on each other for support. A strong sense of a common purpose and a shared determination to achieve EFI status for as many riders as possible was evolving. For me this had become one of the most enriching aspects of the tour. Everyone gave their support freely, sometimes with an act of charity, sometimes with help to change a tube or deal with some other mechanical issue. But more often than not it was just a friendly word of encouragement or a nod to say "I am right there with you".

From the SAG we still had another 35 miles to go to reach the stage finish in Quincy. We clipped in and pedalled out whereupon the skies opened and down came the rain. Big warm droplets of the stuff which bounced off me. Now I guess I was a little premature with yesterday's boast about no rain, but I can say that today's rain was 'nice rain' if there's such a thing. Unlike Britain where the rain is usually cold, the high temperatures and warm road surfaces meant that, for me at least, it didn't detract much from the ride. If anything it improved it by slightly lowering the humidity a tad. I never thought I would claim that rain could improve a ride! Anyway, after a couple of showers, the second of which we sought shelter from in a handy gas station, the roads quickly dried up and blue skies emerged. Apart from slightly squidgy socks and mud-splattered bikes there were no lasting effects.

Milestones two and three came upon us in short order. First up, we crossed the mighty Mississippi River. This marked a critical stage in our journey east. It was both a physical and a mental milestone. The river, the second longest in the country flows for 2,300 miles from Lake Itasca in northern Minnesota to the Gulf of Mexico by New Orleans. The Mississippi River has played a defining role throughout American history, both as a natural barrier and also as a strategic communications and transportation link. In addition to completing 2,000 miles today I also felt a strong sense of progress eastwards. I wondered if now it would be all 'downhill' from here? I very much doubted it!

Our third milestone was passing out of Missouri and into Illinois, the Prairie State, and our eighth state on the tour. As we crossed over, stopping to take a photo of both the state sign and the Quincy city limits sign, we paused to look back at the river. I couldn't help thinking of Paul Robeson's rich baritone voice singing 'Ol' Man River' which contrasts the endless flow of the river with the struggles and hardships of African Americans. Described by many as one of the most hauntingly beautiful songs of the last century, I paused and gathered my own thoughts and reflections once again. I couldn't wait to continue our journey east tomorrow.

Stage 27: Monday 11 June, Quincy to Springfield (107 Miles)

Today marked the fifth century stage of the tour so far and the rumours were that it might be quite tough. In the event it was demanding, but in the Captain's humble opinion, not too tough. As we rolled out of Quincy the omens were uncertain. I spotted a radio mast which disappeared into the low grey clouds that swirled around angrily above us. Rain seemed to be in the air (it stayed dry throughout). We reprised yesterday's cast of riders – The Fabs plus guest artistes. Looking ahead I could see that Person Number Three (Cathy) had fitted a rear mudguard so I wondered if I had made a mistake by sending my Swan Neck, a small mudguard or fender, ahead in the van.

At our pre-stage team meeting this morning, CV and I had decided that today was going to be known as 'Laughter Monday'. After a tough week, spirits in the peloton were flagging somewhat. I felt it was time to lift the mood. To liven up the proceedings, or so I thought, I had bought a $5 air horn during a visit yesterday to a nearby Walmart. I'm not sure if using it actually turned out to be as funny as I had hoped – possibly a case of overkill. Anyway, the laughter started off in fine fettle when one of the faster riders, Barry, who unusually for him was the last to arrive at the start, was told that the rest of us had already gone and he was the last man standing. We were actually hiding around the corner laughing as Barry clipped in and pedalled away. We soon caught him up and he saw the funny side and stayed with us until the first SAG.

Most of today's ride was on State Route 104 E, which had a good surface enabling us to roll along easily. As we were now in Illinois we were surrounded by cornfields (maize) which stretched away for miles on either side of the road. I had been told that this was going to be a common sight for the next several days. The first SAG came up pretty quickly and we pulled over at the St John Wood Community College where the usual fare was on offer, supplemented today by a selection of doughnuts that CV had a weakness for.

Once we were refreshed we set off again bound for the bridge over the Illinois River. The route notes had warned us that there was no shoulder on the bridge so I suspected that I wouldn't be able to get a photo as I crossed it. In the event my luck was in because the traffic was reduced to single file while some road repairs were being carried out. I timed my crossing to the minute and was able to park CV and snatch a pic before the following traffic caught up with me.

While descending the bridge I could see another rider, Mike ahead of me. He had overtaken me while I was taking my photo. As I watched him I noticed something fall out of his jersey pocket and then realised it was his digital camera. Thanks to a short indentation in the bridge wall I was able to pull over, prop CV out of the way and then wait safely until the traffic had passed. Carefully choosing my moment and mimicking the Froomedog's jogging on last year's Ventoux Stage of the Tour de France, I ran back up the bridge to pick up the camera. Then, in double quick time, I legged it back to CV just getting out of the way of the traffic before it swept past me. Sadly the camera had already been crushed by a lorry and I just hoped that the memory card survived so that Mike could retrieve his photos.

After the excitement of my little spot of running I had a fairly hard chase to catch up with the rest of the group. It took me about five miles of fast, hard pedalling to make the catch which I did thanks to temporary traffic lights at some roadworks. Then it was a relatively easy ride to Jacksonville and the second SAG where sweet, cool watermelon was laid on to revive us. We then continued to head east through yet more cornfields before stopping in the intriguingly named New Berlin to get some chocolate milk to boost our energy levels and more water. The village was founded in 1865, not surprisingly by a group of German immigrants. Like many villages we have stopped in, the people here were incredibly friendly.

Entering the gas station in my sweaty and probably quite smelly lycra I could see three very elderly men sitting at a table near the entrance drinking coffee. I was very aware that my arrival had been 'noticed'. I gave them a smile which was met with no response whatsoever. Not even a twitch of face muscles. Looking around the store I could see the chiller cabinets with water and chocolate milk at the back so I made my way over and grabbed my selection. Turning around I looked at the counter where the cash register was and I noticed that the two women there were keeping a close eye on me, I suspect because they were concerned that I might do a runner and make off without paying. I walked over to the counter and I could see them giving me the once over. My dishevelled, mid-afternoon state was clearly not a common sight in these parts. Well, the subsequent conversation went like this.

"Hello, can I pay you for these please?"

"Sure," came the response and I handed over my water, a bottle of chocolate milk and a candy bar.

"Where have you come from?" the counter lady asked me.

A long pause. "I'm sorry I can't remember."

"Where are you going to?"

A longer pause. "I don't know."

By this time the two women were staring at me as if I was the village idiot. The three coffee drinkers were also taking a keen interest in the 'conversation'. Then with a flash of inspiration I blurted out:

"I've come from Los Angeles and I'm riding to Boston."

Well, you could have heard a pin drop before I was asked:

"Are you from Great Britain?" as if that explained everything.

Well to cut a long story short, Bridget, who ran the store quizzed me about the tour and insisted that I came around to her side of the counter to pose for a photo with her and her friend. I sensed that I could have spent all afternoon chatting with my new 'best friends' but I had to take my leave as time was pressing. With a cheery goodbye I made my way to the doorway and the three coffee drinkers wished me well and told me to ride safe. There you have it. The sweaty lycra ice breaker. It works every time. But only with a British accent. Time and time again I have been amazed at how friendly and sincere the people were who I met en route. It really does add an extra level of enjoyment to the riding.

The final leg to Springfield passed without incident. Springfield is the state capital of Illinois and boasts a number of claims to fame. Abraham Lincoln lived here from 1837 to 1861, when he practiced law, before becoming president. His Presidential Library and his tomb are here. The city also played an important role during the Civil War and Colonel Elmer E Ellsworth who was a friend of Lincoln, lived here and was the first Union officer to be killed during the Civil War. He lay in state in the White House and was given a full civic funeral. The cry "Remember Ellsworth" became a rallying call for the Union.

More recently Springfield, Illinois is also reputed to be one of the settings for *The Simpsons*. However, a cursory browse on the Interweb suggested, to me at least, this this might not be quite as clear cut as it seems. Indeed, the programme's creator Matt Groening, muddies the waters with his comments being widely interpreted and, I suspect, misinterpreted. Well, whatever the reality, there seems to be no shortage of entertainment in reading the various theories, and maybe even some conspiracies.

Stage 28: Tuesday 12 June, Springfield to Champaign (89 Miles)

Last night things got a little exciting in Springfield. Around 1:30am I was woken by the sound of thunder and heavy rain falling in the hotel car park. Add a few flashes of lightning and we had a storm. A proper storm! While all this was going on my phone sprang to life as weather warnings were issued. The storm lasted for perhaps an hour. I dozed fitfully through it and several times just when it seemed it might be over, it reprised the action with more rolls of thunder. The sort of thunder that you could hear crashing away across the countryside for miles and miles.

Some mornings when I wake early I have a look at the weather apps on my phone to see what lies in store for us. I'm still using the BBC Weather App which seems to have reasonable coverage of conditions over here. I'm also using another app, AccuWeather, which provides more detailed local information. Yes, like many cyclists I'm a little obsessed with the weather. Having perused the forecasts I also had a peek at the news to discover that Champaign, today's destination, had recently been struck by two minor tornadoes, each lasting less than one minute and registering at the lowest point on the tornado severity index. It seems that there was relatively little damage caused – thankfully.

With the prospect of weather issues on today's ride I decided to play it safe and fitted my Swan Neck mudguard to CV's seatpost. Hopefully if it did rain and the roads were wet I wouldn't suffer from a rain soaked chamois in my shorts! I find that to be particularly unpleasant. Well that and wet socks! Cycling readers will understand the subtleties here!

We said goodbye to Springfield and under grey skies, but with a gentle tailwind, headed off on an initially tricky route making several left and right turns through the suburbs. Once again the 'we' here were The Fabs plus Person Number Three, Nashville Bruce and his chum David who had come down from Chicago for the day to ride with us. After only half a mile I looked back over my shoulder and realised that Pete and Emil weren't visible. I turned around to retrace the route and eventually ran into Pete who mentioned that Emil had had a puncture and had told Pete to go ahead as he would play catch up once he had replaced the tube. The two of us headed off, eventually joining the others at the junction with State Route 54 E. For the record Emil made the catch about 10 miles further up the road.

Now let me tell you about the scenery for most of the rest of the ride. It's quite easy really. Scattered house and farm buildings, a few trees and woods, fields of corn and soya, more fields of corn and soya, lots more fields of corn and soya. Have you got the picture? Yes? Well, unfortunately I didn't as I only took two photos throughout the day – my lowest number on the tour so far.

But it wasn't all boredom. With relatively little traffic and easy spinning we rode two abreast for most of the day, passing the time in conversation with each other. The rough road surface meant we still had to be on guard for potentially wheel buckling potholes – especially as several of them were filled with water from last night's storms. We also had the occasional moment of excitement. At one point we were riding on a long, gently rising straight with occasional traffic coming towards us. Behind me I could hear a truck approaching and dropping down through its gears to wait for a gap in the oncoming traffic before passing us. After about five minutes of this I could hear the truck rev up and start the overtaking manoeuvre.

Here's the thing though. The truck driver needed to work his way through the gears as he picked up speed. However, each gear change resulted in the momentary loss of forward momentum so the overtaking distance required a lot more road. We had even eased the pace slightly to help the truck driver. Up ahead we could see a car approaching and the truck driver started to slow down to pull back in but left it a bit too late. Consequently the oncoming car had to pull off the highway and then off the shoulder and onto the rough gravel roadside fringe, making a fearsome noise, in order to squeeze past. The really surprising thing, however, was that the oncoming car was a Sheriff's vehicle. We fully expected it to turn around, fire up its blues and twos and start chasing. But not a bit of it. Once the road was clear I looked over my shoulder and saw the Sheriff pull back onto the tarmac and continue down the road as if nothing had happened. And, by the way, the lorry passed us too – as soon as the road levelled out.

As this was an 'easy' day we took it at a fairly leisurely pace with two SAGs, at 33 and 64 miles as well as a stop for a drink at a Dairy Queen in between. Bruce had a puncture and Emil had a second one so that all added to the sense of an unhurried ride. The route notes had flagged up a bike shop on the outskirts of Champaign so we pulled over for a look around. Pete got the mechanic to check over his bike – a case of 'if it ain't broke, don't fix it' and Emil got a new rear tyre. I bought a souvenir jersey and some track mitts to replace a pair that have disintegrated!

Now here's the thing. Remember that I said I had fitted my Swan Neck guard to CV before setting off? Did it rain? Yes, bucket loads of the stuff in front and behind us. But did it rain on us? Not a drop! Such is the power of the Swan Neck!

CHAMPAIGN TO ERIE : 7 DAYS, 594 MILES

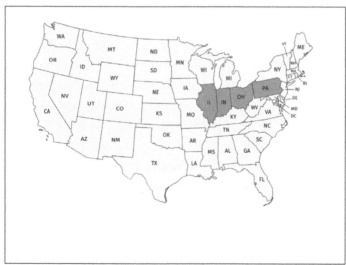

7. ADDING UP THE MILES

Rest Day: Wednesday 13 June, Champaign

I always look forward to our rest days. Don't get me wrong; the riding is as rewarding as ever. The relentless need to keep pushing eastwards is a bit like being on a never-ending conveyor belt. So occasional opportunities to climb off and perhaps even travel backwards are always welcome. As are chances to spend more than one night in the same bed. I have found the daily bed-hopping routine unexpectedly wearing; more so than the riding. This was not something that I had thought about before starting the tour.

Pete and I decided to spend the day exploring Champaign. I had no expectations. Indeed before arriving I hadn't given Champaign a second thought. We spent most of the day in the University District although we did check out a couple of bike shops. This was a delightful campus with nicely landscaped grounds, some outstanding architecture and several lovely art installations. The highlight for me was our visit to the Krannert Art Museum which took a bit of finding but was well worth the effort. The museum was originally completed in 1961 to house the University of Illinois' growing art collection. The distinctive building styled as an acropolis, was designed by the architect Ambrose Richardson who in addition to running his architectural practice, taught in the university. The museum has been extended several times as its collections have grown.

Three of the exhibitions that we looked at illustrated the diversity of approaches that the museum promoted. The first, 'Capturing Landscape', examined the relationship between people and nature through a series of 20th and 21st century black-and-white photographs from the museum's collection. One particular work, 'Manhattan Beach, Looking West from Vista', by Robert Flick was a sequence of small photographs aligned together in a grid which provided a unique, and for me, surprisingly familiar study of the views down the streets running towards the beach. These were the very views that I saw on my first rides in Los Angeles before the tour started. The work evoked some stirring memories and reminded me, once again, just how far I had travelled. Robert Flick has taken the art of photography beyond the limitations of single frame photographs by pioneering the technique of sequential views. With a spot of Giggling on the Interweb and a bit of patience you should also be able to view the work. The necessary clues are all in the preceding words!

By way of a complete contrast, the exhibition, 'And My Mask is Powerful', by Basel Abbas and Ruanne Abou-Rahme was incredibly moving and somewhat unsettling. A video and sound installation presented a group of young people walking through a destroyed village in Palestine and was then followed by a study, a sort of catalogue I suppose, covering the prehistoric past and digital future interpretations of Palestine and the West Bank from a unique perspective. Let me just say that I was really challenged, in a good way, by what I saw and heard. Some of the short writings and poems that were dotted around the installation brought big lumps to my throat. Such power and emotion in the simplicity of the words.

Finally, 'Through the Black Country' by Allan deSouza told the story of an expedition, led by Hafeed Sidi Mubarak Mumbai, to find the elusive source of a fabled river, the Thames. Those familiar with British-African history will recognise the parallels between Livingstone and Stanley and the search for the source of the River Nile. Through photographs, maps and diary entries, the exhibition described the history of London as well as wider contemporary events including a seemingly prophetic account of the great Brexit debacle. The exhibition skilfully straddled the boundaries of fact and fiction to create an engaging and illuminating commentary.

Having more than satisfied our appetites for art, Pete and I adjourned to the nearby Blind Pig Brewery for a welcome couple of beers. Today had been a very enjoyable day and one that was full of unexpected surprises. This is one of the greatest pleasures of a rest day for me. I never quite know what I am going to stumble across. I am usually quite content to explore and discover in a random or spontaneous way as opposed to having a target or a goal to visit a specific place and tick it off a list.

Champaign struck me as a really nice place. There was a real sense of history and atmosphere which made a refreshing change from the concrete installations that the elves construct for us each day. I spotted a couple of pavement bistros and a trattoria and would have liked to have had more time to enjoy them. But the need to ride on eastwards and get back into the bed-hopping routine was upon us once again. Plus ça change!

Stage 29: Champaign to Crawfordsville (82 Miles)

While I spent yesterday being a culture vulture, CV had enjoyed a day of doing absolutely nothing so today we were both ready and rearing to get back on the road. And back on it with a vengeance! Our little group seems to have evolved into the BBC and the Euros. The Fabs seem to have been consigned to history. The BBC are Barry, Bruce and Person Number Three (Cathy). The Euros are Emil, Pete and me. We've been riding together a lot over the last few days, although once we reach the first SAG Barry, who prefers not to linger, usually heads off on his own. The rest of us enjoy a rather more leisurely halt. What I've discovered Americans refer to as lollygagging!

Soon after we rolled out of the hotel Person Number Three and I stopped to photograph some cycling street art followed by a comfort stop (thanks Starbucks). The rest of the group carried on riding and the two of us then engaged in a high-speed pursuit to catch up. Over the next 25 miles, and with a light headwind, we rode hard and fast, going full gas, in an effort to close the gap. We had no idea how big the gap was. We could only guess based on the assumption that the group was maintaining a constant speed and hoping that we were riding 3–4 miles per hour faster than they were. This was hard work, very hard, yet also very satisfying. I led and Kathy pushed me every mile of the way. The further and harder we went I could feel my heart rate rising to a level where I eventually had to back off for fear of popping a rivet or three. And for any cycling readers, yes, I was very definitely 'on the rivet' as cyclists say. Also, as the miles rolled by I could feel the lactate level rising in my legs and I started to wonder how long I could maintain this level of effort. It's been many years since I've ridden a two up time trial in an attempt to sustain such a high output for so long. Nowadays I am much more accustomed to riding at a more moderate speed and at a level of effort that I can maintain for hour after hour.

Eventually, with a long straight road ahead of us I thought I could see a red flashing bike light about half a mile ahead. Resisting the temptation to raise the pace still further, if that were even possible, and risk blowing up, we gradually closed the gap inch by inch, foot by foot over the next couple of miles. Slowly and surely, we pulled them back. With about 400 yards left and with a shout of "Let's go" we stamped on the pedals, Person Number Three came around me and somehow we found the extra 2–3 miles per hour to finally make the catch. Looking at my Strava record that evening I saw that we started chasing at 4.6 miles after the stage start and we eventually made the catch at 29.2 miles and 1 hr 28 minutes after starting the chase. Having joined back on we felt quite entitled to sit on the back and recover. What fun. Hard work but very satisfying, too. I should add that when we reached the SAG my legs cried out "What just happened?" and once I could stand up properly, I had to engage in a spot of leg stretching to untangle my muscles. For the record, CV just purred throughout and took it in her stride.

After the 'excitement' of the first leg we stuck closely together with each of us taking it in turns to lead the group. Shortly after the SAG we crossed the state line into Indiana, the Crossroads of America or alternatively, the Hoosier State. Now we were into the heart of maize growing country with massive fields of green corn stretching as far as the eye could see in every direction. With the temperature rising we paused for a cold drink at a gas station in Veedersburg. Our halt was livened up by the attentions of a couple of passing ladies. They were certainly not backward in coming forward. I am not going to say any more – what goes on tour, stays on tour. But suffice it to say that this wasn't to be the only encounter we had with them today. We began to wonder if they were stalking us! Shortly after starting again we experienced a rare spot of dangerous driving from a passing motorist. We had noticed the driver earlier as he had been pulled over by the Highway Patrol. Person Number Three phoned in our encounter to the local police who said they would follow it up and sure enough a few miles down the road we were passed by a sheriff who acknowledged us and was clearly looking for the wayward motorist. I very much doubted that a similar report would have produced the same response back home in the UK.

Our spirits were soon restored though. Approaching the village of Hillsboro the threshold sign proclaimed that Hillsboro was the 'Home of 600 Happy People and a few Old Soreheads'! That's quite a claim. Hillsboro was originally established around 1820 and over the subsequent years became a local centre for grist and textile milling. At its peak the mill worked double shifts. Sadly, like many small villages in this part of Indiana, the village never really prospered and the community reduced to its present size as other neighbouring villages and towns assumed precedence. No matter though, at least the folk here were happy and I didn't see any soreheads. The final leg to Crawfordsville passed without incident and it was one weary Captain who finally collapsed onto the armchair in his hotel room. But one happy Captain too.

Stage 30: Friday 15 June, Crawfordsville to Indianapolis (55 Miles)

Today was another short day and the ride over to Indianapolis was pretty unremarkable. So unremarkable that I had only taken one photograph until the last leg of the stage. But it was definitely worth the wait. If I tell you that on the first half of the route we passed through endless fields of maize and soya along straight, nondescript roads, you'll probably get the picture. The tedium was lifted slightly in Jamestown where we spotted a large white metal statue of a figure striding across the grass. Quick as a flash Pete had us doing a variation of the Madness walk to lighten the mood. And if I've lost you here look for Madness (the band) videos on You Tube and work it out for yourself!

We approached the outskirts of Indianapolis on some very busy and very rough roads. It was all rather unpleasant riding. But with a few miles to stage end it all changed for the better. Leaving the main roads we initially turned onto the Eagle Creek Cycle Trail which led us onto the White River Whapahani Trail and it was like crossing over into a new world. Gone were the noisy, exhaust-fume belching lorries passing through an endless series of industrial areas. Now we had entered utopia or so it seemed. The Miami Tribe, not to be confused with

151

their Florida counterparts (the Mayaimi) were one of the Great Lakes tribes who gave the river its name, Whapahani meaning 'White Sands' or Waapi-nipi Siipiiwi, meaning 'White Lake River'.

A lovely smooth tarmac cycle trail wove its way through mature trees and woods with glimpses of the White River beyond. In just a few seconds we were in a magical world, quite lush and teeming with wildlife. The transformation was total and totally unexpected. Although we had been given a heads up at the morning's route rap nothing had prepared me for this experience.

But there was more to come. We burst out of the trees onto a small promontory with the whole of downtown Indianapolis laid in front of us. The modern skyscrapers sitting on the horizon with the river cascading over some rapids in front of us was just magnificent. Although this had been only a short part of the whole stage it easily made up for the underwhelming nature of the previous parts.

Gradually we got nearer and nearer to the city centre, turning eventually onto a wide car-free bridge to cross the river. The White River State Park that we had been riding through is one of the jewels in the city's crown. It is very pedestrian and cyclist friendly and, for me a least, quite different to anything I had seen so far on the tour. The range of street art provided a vivid contrast to some of the city's buildings, many of which are architectural masterpieces. Although in European terms they are relatively recent constructions, many of the buildings are very traditional in their design with huge columns and pillars enriched with intricate stonework.

The last few miles were so enthralling that I seized an entirely unexpected opportunity to ride it again with Mary who needed to find a bike shop to repair one of her brake levers which had broken. We backtracked the route and made our way to a bike shop that I had noticed earlier. Unfortunately, despite their best efforts they were unable to make an effective repair, which meant that Mary would have to order a replacement lever to be fitted further along the route. Despite this setback, Mary hid her disappointment well and we made the most of the cycle path back to the hotel. As we rode along together I recalled a song, 'These Are the Days' by Van Morrison which perfectly summed up how I felt about today's ride. Van urges us to savour, enjoy and hold days like this in our hearts. As the end of the tour slowly comes onto the horizon I found that increasingly I was taking stock and reflecting on those moments, places and people that I will be holding in my heart. This was very definitely one of them.

Arriving at tonight's hotel I had quite a surprise. I found that I had been allocated a suite. Well, more of an apartment really with a lounge, dining area complete with table and chairs to seat eight, kitchen, large double bedroom, a bathroom with a separate jacuzzi. And, opening one of the internal doors, I found some stairs leading down to a swimming pool. Wow what luxury. It was such a shame that I was only there for one night! After a spell in the jacuzzi I enjoyed sitting on the balcony and looking out over the canal below, complete with a gondola. Dinner that evening at a nearby Italian restaurant was, for a change, very appetising. Mary and I enjoyed a brief walk around Monument Circle after dinner. The 284 feet high obelisk styled Soldiers and Sailors Monument was publicly dedicated in 1902 and looking at it and the piazza I almost felt that I had been transported to Italy; Rome or Florence maybe. The neo-classically styled Hilbert Circle Theatre which was built in 1916 added to the Italian feeling. As we walked back to the hotel, Van Morrison's words played in my head again. Savour, enjoy, hold!

Stage 31: Saturday 16 June, Indianapolis to Richmond (72 Miles)

With the prospect of three tough days ahead, today was another relatively easy stage and BBC and the Euros rolled out of Indianapolis bound for Richmond. I was rather fetchingly kitted out (well I thought so) in a new orange and blue Illinois Fighting Illini college jersey that I bought on our last rest day in Champaign. Rather frustratingly I had a puncture within the first five miles – another of those infernal truck tyre wires. Fortunately the team rallied round and the tube change was made in very short order. An added bonus was that with impeccable timing Mary, who was driving one of the support vehicles today, pulled up with a track pump at exactly the right moment. In less than five minutes I was rolling down the road again. Having a puncture in the first few miles of a stage can often set the tone for the remainder of the day so I was delighted not to suffer any further misfortunes. Indeed today was a very relaxed, almost leisurely affair with several stops for photos and refreshments as well as some good-natured chit-chat in between.

Passing through Greenfield at about 20 miles, guess who I spotted sitting on bench? James Whitcomb Riley, the well-known Hoosier poet, author and entertainer. So I pulled over for a chat with him. Now I guess I ought to come clean at this point. When I say that I pulled over for a chat with James, I am talking metaphorically, not literally. He was born in Greenfield in 1849 and now his statue sits gracefully on a bench on the sidewalk surveying all who pass by. Riley's career received an early boost with an endorsement from Henry Wandsworth Longfellow (author of *The Song of Hiawatha*) and his most famous works include *Little Orphant Annie* and *The Raggedy Man,* the latter providing the inspiration for the Raggedy Ann doll, beloved of many children.

Hoosier incidentally is the collective name for the inhabitants of Indiana – hence Indiana is known as the Hoosier State. The source of the name is uncertain but it was in common use by the 1840s. Sadly, the term is also used in a rather more derogatory fashion, which I am not going to get into here.

Every so often on a ride you get an entirely unexpected surprise. Riding in one direction, looking ahead, means that I often failed to spot a sight or feature. But sometimes you get dealt a lucky hand as I did today. With hot, humid conditions we pulled into a gas station in Cambridge City to get a cold drink. Cambridge City, which is named after the university city near where I live in the east of England seemed a nice place. With the number of Stars and Stripes flags and banners on display along the Main Street it was clearly a patriotic place. It was apparently also a highly popular place for antique collectors to visit. Well, while downing my drink on the gas station forecourt I happened to look back towards the direction we had come from and right in front of me was a magnificent mural. Not just any mural either but a depiction of Abraham Lincoln's funeral train which transported the late President's coffin from Washington DC to Springfield, Illinois. The train passed slowly through Cambridge City at 4:15am on 30 April, 1865. Although not scheduled to make any official stops it did in fact stop three times in Cambridge. The first lasted 5 seconds outside the home of General Meredith, a friend and ally of Lincoln, where the whistle was sounded in tribute. Then the train stopped a second time for 15 seconds at the grand arch in the city centre so that 3,000 townspeople could pay their respects. Finally the train stopped at a level crossing on the western edge of the city, though I am not sure why. The larger than life mural, by Pamela Bliss, was unveiled in April 2015 to mark the 150th anniversary of Lincoln's death. This was part of a bigger commemoration of the event when the entire city was decked out in mourning, just as it was a century and a half before. It just goes to show that sometimes it is well worth looking over your shoulder.

From Cambridge City to Richmond was an easy spin. And Pete and I paused for the usual stage end photos in front to the town sign. And, no we didn't have to look over our shoulders; we saw it coming!

Stage 32: Sunday 17 June, Richmond to Marysville (104 Miles)

Today's stage was another century ride, the first of three in succession. We rolled out of Richmond and three miles up the road crossed the state line into Ohio, the tenth state on the tour so far. I had heard that this part of Ohio, the Buckeye State, was very pretty so I was looking forward to the ride. The countryside here was very lush and green with lots of trees, hedges and woods set in rolling land. In places it felt very much like parts of where I live in Suffolk, especially the area to the east of Newmarket so I felt quite at home. After seeing my photos of the day, one of my riding chums back at home said just that in a message to me!

One of the challenges I have riding in countryside like this is the difficultly of concentrating on the Garmin and the route map. It is all too easy to get so absorbed in the passing scenery and miss a critical turn. The Garmin responds almost immediately with an 'off course message' but if you are not looking at it then you are none the wiser. And yes, I'll fess up now. I once went several miles before I realised the error of my navigation.

But it's not all doom and gloom Sometimes going the wrong way reveals a hidden delight. Today was a case in point. Having missed a right-hand turning I spotted an old mill building ahead of me so I rode over to investigate. And what a lovely four storey wooden building it was. Complete with a replica vintage pickup truck parked outside. Built in 1849 by Gabriel Baer, Bear's Mill is now one of the last operating water-powered mills in Ohio. The original hand-hewn timber beams are still visible in the building. The external woodwork clapperboards are constructed from Black Walnut. The millrace, which provides the power source for the mill, was constructed by school children who were paid 50 cents a day for their labour. Over the next century the mill changed hands several times. In 1947, Charles Andrews acquired the mill. In addition to being a pioneering environmentalist he was also a leading advocate of health food. One of his most notable achievements was developing a market for organic grain and flour. His products were exported around the globe at a time when the organic movement was in its infancy.

Today the mill is owned by the Friends of Bear Mill, a charity. Their work enables visitors to learn about the history of the mill through guided tours. Displays celebrate food, nature and art and the small store has a tantalising mix of flours, gourmet foods, coffee, clothing and jewellery. An art gallery displays the paintings, sculpture, pottery and photography of artists from the Ohio Valley. This was another example of a totally unexpected surprise. And a reminder that getting lost or straying from our intended route, can bring its own delights.

There wasn't much to trouble me physically on today's stage. It was largely flat with smooth surfaces and fast tarmac. We did, however, come across a couple of disruptions – some road resurfacing works and a collapsed bridge both of which we took in our stride. Literally as we dismounted, shouldered our bikes and walked across the unrideable bits. Nothing stops us!

Our SAG stops usually provide a welcome interlude to each day's stage. They enable us to refuel and refill our water supplies. More often than not they are places where we get together and chat, sharing and exchanging our perspectives on the ride so far and sometimes engage in debates to solve world-class problems. The availability of a restroom is a key consideration, especially for the female riders on the tour. For the men, if the essential facilities are lacking then a strategically located tree or bush will usually suffice. Today's second SAG was in a large parking lot in the city of Urbana. With no restroom within close walking distance, Adam walked over to some mature trees a reasonable distance away to discretely seek his relief. Relief obtained, as he was strolling back across the parking lot he was confronted by a highly irate man who clearly took exception to Adam's actions and started telling him so in no uncertain terms. The rest of us, standing some distance away, looked on ready to intervene if events took a turn for the worse. Adam is a tall, lithe and very mild-mannered person not given to causing offence. In a masterstroke of diplomacy, he stood stationary as his aggressor let forth. At the same time Adam calmly reached behind is jersey, extracted a banana from his pocket and proceeded to peel and eat it, all without saying one word. Viewed from a couple of hundred yards away the scene was almost comical. Eventually the complainant ran out of steam and walked off muttering darkly about "those rude cyclists". Adam on the other hand finished his banana, carefully folded up the skin and discarded it in a nearby dustbin. Job done, as they say!

One hundred and five miles and exactly six hours after setting off Pete and I rolled into Marysville. This was the first of four successive long riding days – I can sense the possibilities of another century on tomorrow's stage and possibly one even the day after. CV is liking this. My legs are not so sure!

Every evening in the reception area of our hotel a large map is displayed showing how far we have come. Since leaving Los Angeles last month we have travelled about 2,600 miles and have passed through nine states. I remember looking at the map a few days after we set off and thinking that, although we had pedalled a lot a lot of miles, the map made it look as if we hadn't travelled very far. Looking at the map when we arrived in Marysville today after a long and hot stage I realised that we have made huge progress. The line tracing our route, and the photographs along it, show just how far we have come. What really struck me today was that we really are closer, much closer to the end now. There are only eleven riding days left until we reach the east coast and dip our wheels in the Atlantic Ocean.

I'm looking at this with very mixed feelings. Satisfaction and a growing feeling of achievement as we get ever closer to the finishing line. Not that I'm counting any chickens. Happiness at the new friendships I've made, including a couple of very special ones which I hope will continue after the tour. Pride at being part of a group of riders who together have grown into a magnificent and strongly supportive team. The collective response to overcoming the interstate puncture challenge set, for me at least, a new benchmark in teamwork. And with the departure and whitewashing of most of the tour support crew we have achieved a fabulous level of rapport and respect amongst the riders.

Of course a lot can happen in the eleven days that remain. And I am sure that my thoughts and reflections will continue to evolve but today's stage was, for me, one of reflecting and taking stock. It was a stage that a close friend of mine would really have liked to have ridden. For me it had a certain English countryside feel to it and I would have enjoyed chatting about what we saw. So, my motivator for riding today was my 'absent' friend. There in my thoughts throughout the day if not in person.

Stage 33: Monday 18 June, Marysville to Wooster (100 miles)

The cue sheet for today showed that the stage was 97 Miles. Close, temptingly close, to a century. But 97 miles, or even 99.9 miles, doesn't qualify as a century. It was game on for a few extra miles at the end of the stage to rack up a proper century and get three in succession. As I set off I wondered what surprises might lie in store for me today. Little did I know!

The stage was another full day's riding in Ohio. As we progressed eastwards the countryside was getting more and more lush. Lots of greenery; grass, crops, trees, hedges, woods and forests. Delightful roads meandering through valleys with gurgling and bubbling streams and rivers, some full of fish. Lots of lovely properties too, large and small, mostly set back from the roads and almost invariably well maintained. The homes of proud folk. And lots of architecturally simple, plain white churches. It was totally enjoyable riding, and I was often able to freewheel along as I took it all in and soaked up everything around me.

About halfway along the stage I had one unexpected and very pleasant encounter. I had stopped at a bridge to get a picture of the river we had been following for several miles and while looking around a woman, in her late thirties I guessed, and driving a Land Rover Discovery, stopped and asked me if everything was okay. Replying in the affirmative, I complemented her on her choice of (British) vehicle and added that I was just admiring the view. Picking up on my accent she got out of the vehicle, asked if I would like a drink of cold water and walked over, clearly wanting to chat. I learned that she lived nearby in Bellville and was on her way back from Perrysville, which I was heading towards, and where her sister had been looking after her kids for the day. She was fascinated by my tour and bombarded me with questions about it. In the course our conversation I also learned that she was a long-distance cyclist, mostly one day and weekend tours, and had a long-held ambition to ride a USA coast-to-coast tour. She told me that she had had to put her ambitions on hold while she was bringing up her children but hoped to be able to do the tour in a few years. As we were chatting there was a cry from the back of her car to which she said, "Oh that's just one of my kids waking up." Sensing that our conversation was coming to an end I mentioned my blog site to which she produced a pen and paper and got me to write down the URL. She told me her name was Susan and that she would follow my progress avidly. So Susan, in the unlikely event that you read my writings here I say "thank you" for your concern, interest and friendship. One again I was struck by the kindness of strangers which so enriched my riding.

Today, the character of the route changed towards the back end. A complete transformation from gentle undulations to rollers. And some quite brutal rollers at that. Around about the 70-mile mark we faced a succession of climbs, some touching 12 per cent, which had me changing down onto the granny ring that I haven't needed to use for some time. With the temperature and humidity rising sharply, what had seemed like an easy ride turned into something much more challenging. Now it was almost a case of survival. I could feel the seemingly never-ending succession of rollers leaching away the strength from my legs. The downhill sections provided opportunities to recover but never quite enough before the road turned upwards again.

The high humidity was really strength sapping. I spotted one rider who, for fear of overheating, had taken shelter in a roadside barn in an attempt to cool down. Fortunately, relief was on hand as Mary had set up an impromptu water station shortly after the village of Blachleyville. The scene was really quite surreal as rider after rider descended on the SAG vehicle to slake their thirst. Although we were only ten miles from the stage end, I was sure that without the opportunity to hydrate, several riders, including me, would have been in serious difficulty.

I did have one moment of light relief as I arrived at the village of Funk. Yes, that's right, there is actually a village called 'Funk'. By coincidence as I was taking the requisite photo Mary and Navi, a rider who today was sagging, pulled up and quick as a flash Navi worked her magic and a burst of James Brown emerged from the car's speakers. Well, I didn't need a second call. My legs got moving, my body got shimmying and I gave it my all to the beat. Fortunately, this time no photos or videos exist! You will have to take it from me – I was funky in Funk!

The last part of the stage into Wooster was relatively straightforward. Pete and I eased into town via a rather fine bike shop – we didn't buy anything. Then with a couple of circuits of the town to put on the requisite miles for the century we rolled up at our hotel just as the clouds burst – literally. Two centuries in two days – wonderful.

My reverie was soon shattered though when Mary sent me a text asking me to come and see her as soon as possible. I was shocked to discover that she had become the latest victim of the whitewashing treatment metered out by the tour organisers. Seemingly her work to support a group of riders a few days earlier by ensuring they were able to eat their dinner when they wanted to, had met with the organisers' disapproval. It appeared that Mary had been penalised for doing the very thing that she was there to do. Support us, the riders. And support us in a way that I believe all of us, the riders, felt she did outstandingly.

Our friendship had grown since Robin had been whitewashed from the tour in St. Joseph on Stage 23. I was so appalled at the treatment Mary had received that I spent a long evening and night struggling to decide whether or not I really wanted to continue with the tour myself. To her credit, Mary talked me out of such thoughts and encouraged me to continue riding and complete my EFI. Although I had been enjoying the riding and the camaraderie of the other riders, aspects of the logistical support were beginning to wear me down. But eventually I resolved not to be beaten.

We enjoyed a lovely candlelit dinner together in a delightful bistro in Wooster. It was especially nice to eat fresh food which tasted like it had been prepared to order, rather than the more usual manufactured fodder that the chain eateries provide. For Mary, leaving had become something of a release too. I hadn't fully realised the pressure she been under as a consequence of the demands and attitudes of the tour organisers. And, as it transpired, Mary had been able to arrange an impromptu reunion with Robin and together they would be spending several days on their own mini-tour in New England. From our subsequent phone calls over the following days I could hear the New England enjoyment in Mary's voice with lots of laughter thrown in. I christened Mary and Robin 'the cycling sisters' and wished I was there with them sharing in the fun.

Stage 34: Tuesday 19 June, Wooster to Niles (102 Miles)

It was with a heavy heart that I said my goodbyes to Mary after breakfast with the promise of meeting her again in Boston at the end of the tour. CV and I rolled out of Wooster at the usual time of 7:30am and gradually headed eastwards on a succession of quiet country roads. For the first hour or so I was very tempted to turn around and head back to Wooster. But Mary's encouragement and her wise words resonated in my head, if not in my heart. Several other riders, realising what had happened, were very considerate and asked me to pass on their good wishes and thoughts to Mary. The Euros, Pete and Emil, were hugely supportive too. They didn't say much but I could sense their feelings of care, concern and support. And as for CV, well she was the best friend I could hope for in such trying circumstances.

The countryside we passed through was beautiful. The further east we progressed the lusher it seemed to get. We crossed over a large lake before entering Berlin (not that one!). The village was founded in 1816 by John Swigert who, not surprisingly, came from the other Berlin. Most of the early inhabitants were from

163

Germany and Switzerland. Today, the village is best known as the largest Amish community in Ohio.

Leaving the village I spotted a depot full of yellow school buses and I pulled over to grab a photo. It's not often that I've seen such a big nest of buses! The seemingly deserted bus compound was fenced off and I spent some time trying to work out how to get inside with CV. I figured that there was chance to snag a truly iconic photo and I was not going to pass up the opportunity lightly. A sixth sense, a last glance over my shoulder before I engaged in a spot of breaking and entering, proved to be my savour. Looking back, I spotted a Sheriff's vehicle with a deputy sitting inside watching me closely. With as much nonchalance as I could muster I rode over to him and asked if I could lean CV on the front of his vehicle for a photo. After looking up and down at me he said it would be okay. With the photo taken I thanked him and we then engaged in a lengthy discussion about how American motorists treated cyclists compared to those in the UK. The deputy had quite a few interesting opinions, and I suspect that on the basis of my observations about UK motorists, he may now think that I come from a country of homicidal drivers. "How close do they pass you? Wow!" And for the record I was positive about my own experiences of American motorists on the tour. Time was pressing on and the stage finish at Niles beckoned so I had to leave my peacekeeping friend to his peacekeeping duties and resume the ride eastwards. By way of a farewell the deputy commented that he was glad that I didn't try to get into the bus depot. Otherwise would have been having a rather different conversation!

The final part of the ride was a real delight – a dedicated paved cycle route through the woods to the edge of Niles. It was a really blissful experience. So lovely that I actually turned around and rode back a few miles to do it again, using the time to clear my head and float free! I also had a hidden agenda. The extra miles meant that by the time I arrived at the hotel I had managed to notch up my third successive century! Yay.

It was a great disappointment not to see Mary at the hotel that evening. We had a lengthy phone conversation when I learned that she had rented a car and was now on her way to Boston to meet Robin. Hearing the relief and happiness in her voice at escaping from the petty power politics of the tour organisers gave me a great boost. And by all accounts, Robin was arranging a great self-supported tour in New England in a couple of days' time.

Stage 35: Wednesday 20 June, Niles to Erie (90 Miles)

I awoke the following morning to a leaden grey, heavy sky. Rain was in the air. So on with the Swan Neck to protect my backside from the spray. The last time I fitted it, no rain had fallen so I was hoping it would work in my favour today. Sadly it didn't and within just a few miles the heaven's opened, down came the rain and on went my Castelli Idrio jacket (100 per cent breathable, 100 per cent waterproof). Breathability was a major consideration with the high humidity we have been experiencing these last few days. Sadly, the rain stayed with us until virtually the end of the stage so I just got on with it, tapping out the miles one by one. Pete, who had been experiencing some knee troubles over the last couple of days, had decided to leave with the earlier group as he fancied a gentler day on the road. This was the first time I rode without him since we rode together in California on our Hollywood jaunt. Was it something I said? Pete assured me it wasn't!

Our first SAG was in the village of Andover which has its origins in the early nineteenth century with the arrival of the railway. The first settlers were from Connecticut and seem to have brought the Andover name with them. One of the first settlers was Col. William Morley whose son, Byron, published *The Enterprise*, the local newspaper. Byron was quite an entrepreneur and also owned the post office, drug store, general store, a cheese factory, and a monumental mason's works. A school was established in 1814 and a Presbyterian Church followed in 1818. A large part of the town was destroyed by a fire in 1890 which led to the creation of a volunteer fire department. There was also an Opera House which was where James Garfield, later to become the 20th President of United States, was thrown down the stairs because he backed the women's suffrage movement. Garfield only served six months in office before being assassinated in 1881. I found it fascinating that the further east we rode, modern American history went further back in time.

We sheltered in the lee of a McDonalds drive-thru in the forlorn hope that the rain would ease before steeling ourselves to start riding again with the goal of getting to the second SAG as quickly as possible. What followed was a 20-mile ride along a straight road with torrential rain falling into our faces and a road surface covered with puddles and sheets of water that hid potentially wheelbucking potholes in the tarmac. Each of us had to hang back to avoid being showered with spray from the rider immediately in front. Get too close, as I did several times and I could hear the spray drops battering the lenses of my riding glasses. The only consolation was that the route profile was predominantly downhill which made the riding marginally easier.

After about 90 minutes of riding in these challenging conditions the rain eased and we turned eastwards just before reaching the shores of Lake Erie. Sweet relief was at hand, too, in the shape of the White Turkey Drive-in, an establishment which has achieved legendary status on previous tours. It was founded in 1952 by Eddie and Marge Tuttle as a place to showcase their farm-raised turkey sandwiches. The restaurant took its name from the White Holland breed of turkey. The business is still run by the family and their friends. But I had heard of something else that they served which I had decided to try. A root beer float which, when it arrived was so large that I was left wondering if I was meant to share it despite asking for the small size! Under the expert tutelage of Bruce, who I had been riding with, I stirred with my spoon and pushed with my straw and got stuck in. Now I have to say that root beer is an acquired taste and with a little practice it is a taste that I might well acquire – especially when the float is so delicious. As I downed the drink and spooned the icecream I could see Bruce looking at me out of the corner of his eye and smiling to himself. You may just have started something Sir Bruce!

Once the root beer float was downed, or even drowned, and despite the cessation of the rain I kept the Idrio on and crossed over into Pennsylvania (state number 10). Pennsylvania is known as The Keystone State because it was the middle state of the original thirteen founding states of the United States, and also because it has held a key position in the economic, social, and political development of the United States. The state threshold sign proudly proclaimed that: "Pennsylvania was founded in 1681 by William Penn as a Quaker Commonwealth. Birthplace of The Declaration of Independence and The Constitution of the United States." And don't forget Lincoln's Gettysburg address: "Four score and seven years ago our fathers brought forth on this continent, a new nation, conceived in Liberty, and dedicated to the proposition that all men are created equal..."

With that foretaste of history we rolled on and into Erie and the prospect of a day off the saddle. I arrived with a dry backside and body (thanks Swan Neck and Idrio) but as I walked into the foyer of the hotel I could hear my feet squelching. Ah well, everyone can't be perfect I suppose. Erie had the feel of a really nice place and the hotel was situated right on the lakeshore. And, I hoped an ideal place to have a proper rest and recharge my batteries after the tumultuous events of the last few days.

ERIE TO BOSTON : 8 DAYS, 580 MILES

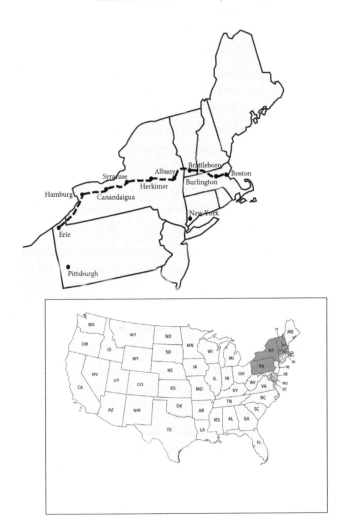

8. THE CAPTAIN IS COMING

Rest Day: Thursday 21 June, Erie

After an evening spent imbibing rather a lot of beer, today got off to a slow start. Pete and I walked into the city centre along the waterfront and then up to Perry Square Park where we spotted Dave's Diner, found a booth and enjoyed a head clearing brunch, or for those in the know a 'Full English'. With seemingly never-ending refills of coffee we were soon firing on all cylinders. After a walk around the Park and a quick look around the Art Museum we headed back towards the lake shore to visit the Maritime Museum which we had spotted earlier.

The Museum which opened in 1988 and was previously an electricity generating plant, presents Erie's role in the history of the of the Great Lakes. Its main focus is the War of 1812 between the United States and Great Britain. This arose because of economic sanctions imposed by Britain and France as part of the Napoleonic Wars. From our visit to the museum I learnt that the Napoleonic conflict had extended beyond Europe and across the Atlantic. The centrepiece of the museum, though, was a replica of the US Brig *Niagara*, Commodore Perry's flagship in the Battle of Lake Erie in 1813. In a dramatic turn of events late in the battle, nine US Navy ships, led eventually by the Niagara, defeated and captured six British vessels thereby ensuring American control of the lake for the rest of the war. The current replica, the third one to be built, dates from 1988 and is now used for sail training. As we looked on from the quayside we could see a group of young people learning some of the necessary skills for handling a square-rigged ship like this.

By mid-afternoon our energy levels were subsiding and we returned to the hotel for a siesta. I also used the time to give CV a thorough going over including a full wash and wax. She has been enjoying our tour and has been an outstanding companion. Apart from the brake issue before Santa Fe she hasn't experienced any injuries and, like me, is eagerly looking forward to the last phase of the tour.

During this morning's investigation of Erie I had spotted an eating establishment that seems to be quite rare in the USA. A curry house. Readers who know me will know that I have a weakness for Indian food so the chance to assault my taste buds with an assortment of spices was not one I was going to pass up. Rod, who comes from Colorado Springs and is one of the Three Amigos, joined us to sample the fare. The Tandoori Hut did not let us down. My go-to curry is a Chicken Jalfrezi and the one I sampled here certainly met my expectations. With steamed rice, some lentils and a roti I felt rejuvenated and ready to hit the road tomorrow.

Stage 36: Friday 22 June Erie to Hamburg (81 Miles)

This morning started with the daily kitbag battle. I must be losing my touch because one of the kitbags stubbornly refused to zip shut. This was mostly because I had acquired some extra rations. Robin had sent a box of energy bars and other delicacies to the hotel in Erie as a morale booster for Mary, who like me, had been finding the standard fare somewhat underwhelming. What Robin couldn't have known was that by the time I reached Erie Mary would also have been whitewashed. So it fell to me to retrieve the package and Mary told me to make free with the contents. Eventually with some crafty actions, including filling my training shoes with some of the energy bars, I managed to tug the zip shut.

Looking at the map I could see that most of today's route ran parallel to the southern shore of Lake Erie so I was hoping for some good photo opportunities. State Route 5 heads gradually north east with occasional glimpses of the lake through the trees. As we rode out of Erie, Bruce pointed out a sign commemorating Captain C. V. Grindley. So this Captain, riding a CV, just had to take the picture. The other Captain was an officer in the US Navy during the American Civil War. He was stationed in Erie between 1871 and 1875. He subsequently served in the Philippines before contracting dysentery and possibly liver failure which led to his death in June 1898. He was buried in Erie's Lakeside Cemetery.

Around the 20-mile point we crossed over into the Empire State, New York. This was a landmark moment for me and a realisation that the end of the tour was not far away now. The thought of entering a state that has its eastern edge on the Atlantic Ocean really did bring it home to me. I spent quite a few minutes thinking about what this meant. Seven weeks in the saddle on tour is a long time and I have to say that while I was still in good shape physically the succession of one-night stays and the conveyor belt of chain eatery food was taking its toll. Fortunately for me the highs of riding more than compensate for the domestic challenges – most of the time. Of course it isn't over until the fat lady sings. But today I sent word to the good people of Boston, through Mary and Robin, that the Captain was coming. He was riding hard and fast and there will be fireworks, music and maybe even a dance when he arrives. Indulge me here readers; indulge me!

What had been a complete surprise to me were the numerous vineyards that lined the road for the first half of the stage. Pennsylvania is the largest grape-growing region in the country after California and the Lake Erie area is known as 'the Grape Belt of America'. Over two dozen grape varieties are grown here including native reds (Catawba and Concord) and whites (Niagara), as well as a large number of hybrid species (Baco Noir, Seyval Blanc). There are also several European varieties such as Cabernet Sauvignon, Merlot, Pinot Grigio and Chardonnay. I could see that the soil was suitable but I was surprised that the climate was favourable as I would have thought spring frosts might be a problem but clearly not; perhaps due to the lake's microclimate. Vines have been grown in the state since 1683. The wine growing region has over 200 wineries, including several with an international reputation and others where a new generation of winemakers are challenging tradition, with some success.

Now I'd like to let you into a little secret. Well, two secrets. Today I rode through Barcelona and also through Dunkirk on the way to our destination at Hamburg. That must be some sort of record for crossing Europe, surely. Barcelona refers to the harbour in the town of Westfield and its most notable feature is the 40-foot tall lighthouse which was constructed in 1829 and was the first in the world to be powered by natural gas. Dunkirk is named after its French counterpart also has a lighthouse, built in 1826. And as for Hamburg. Well that's a story for tomorrow!

Returning to the subject of records for a moment, I was pleased to see that I had claimed a Strava KOM (King of the Mountains) on the Southwestern Rollers segment (4.7 miles). At the time of achieving my record I lead the field by over a minute but I'm guessing that I won't be out in front for very long. But let me enjoy the moment, please!

The first half of the ride was really enjoyable with a reasonable road surface, attractive scenery and relatively little traffic competing for the tarmac space. Unfortunately the second half was much less pleasant – the wide shoulder was definitely needed given the increased volume of traffic. I rode into Hamburg with Chris who is from Manchester and now lives in Florida and is relatively new to cycling – golf is his thing and very good he is at it too. But I have to tell you that Chris is also a source of great inspiration. Every single day since leaving Los Angeles, Chris has ridden to the limit and has been determined to make it to the finish. Chris has a rare and currently incurable cancer, a lymphoma. Aside from the personal challenge, he is riding to raise funds for research into the cancer. I felt very privileged and honoured to ride alongside him for a while today and share our tour perspectives. Compared to Chris, my struggles are trivial.

Once I had finished the stage I had an opportunity to tick off another item from my 'to do' list. Emil and his wife Eve invited Pete and me to join them on an excursion to see Niagara Falls. Although this was a very brief visit I was glad to have made it. The Falls were everything that had I hoped they would be and it was quite mesmerising watching the power of the water as it made its way over the edge. It was a great way to end the day. Rumour had it that tomorrow was going the be a tough day so I headed to bed early.

Stage 37: Saturday 23 June, Hamburg to Canandaigua (96 Miles)

Well here we are, another day nearer the end with a long stage across upstate New York. Now here's a thing I didn't know. There's the town of Hamburg which was established by decree in 1812. One of the earliest recorded events was agreement to place a $5 bounty on wolf hides due to complaints by local people. But in addition to the town there is also a quite separate village of Hamburg which spun off from the town in 1874. That explained the sign I saw on the way out!

Today was clearly going to be a signs day as I saw references to Warsaw and Lima as well as Wales. Naturally I stopped to get a photograph of the latter. Established in 1818, the town of Wales was given its name because the green fields and hills reminded the founders of the land of my fathers. I understand that the townspeople work hard to preserve a smalltown, traditionalist atmosphere with much emphasis being placed on family life and small business. It bills itself as "a town of families, friends, farms and so much more!" To celebrate the town's bicentennial this year, a wide range of events were being staged including walks, sports events, a potluck picnic and intriguingly a pie baking contest with the entries being judged a couple of weeks after I passed through. The pies, all of the dessert variety, needed to be entirely homemade and have at least a pastry base. Where I come from, a pie without a top crust is actually a tart and not a pie. All entrants had to provide two identical pies; one to be judged and one to the auctioned. Points were going to be awarded for overall taste, presentation, crust, and filling flavour. I imagined that this was going to be a fiercely contested event and I wondered who would win. I am always fascinated by the diverse events and activities I come across on my rides that towns and villages organise to foster community spirit. This was no exception.

Heading onwards from Wales I found myself riding with Person Number Three. With the rain of the last few days the road surfaces have collected a lot of debris and unfortunately for Cathy this translated into three punctures in rapid succession. On the second occasion we pulled up on the drive of a local house owner who soon appeared with her dog to see if she could help. In short order we learnt that Kathy was also a cyclist, that her husband races and that her dog was called Thor. As is usually the case on these occasions we had an interesting chat about our tour and, Kathy, if you are reading this please accept our grateful thanks for your assistance. You are another shining example of the kindness of strangers.

Person Number Three had her third puncture just before the first SAG of the day so we decided to replace the tyre with a new one – no punctures for her thereafter. The first SAG marked another significant milestone in our journey eastwards; we had reached the 3,000-mile point. There are now just 417 miles to go to the Atlantic Ocean. I can't believe how much has happened in the last six weeks. Person Number Three and I rode out of the SAG together pretty smartly as she was hoping to link up with some friends who had set out from the second SAG and were riding back towards us. Link up we soon did to huge whoops of delight from Person Number Three and her friends. As soon as they had turned around and completed the introductions I managed to bring the party atmosphere to a halt with my own rear wheel puncture. This was only a short-lived distraction though and we were soon underway again.

The second SAG was in the town of Avon at the volunteer fire station where the restrooms have been used for several years by the tour. The fire station is not usually manned and the fire master leaves the side door unlocked and we just enter and do what we have to do. I had a quick look around the inside of the station and managed to snag a pic of CV and me propped up against one of the engines.

We headed off on the final leg. Today had the feel of a sluggish ride. I guess that the accumulated mileage was starting to take its toll – on some more than others. Bruce is wearing compression socks at night and packs his knee with ice as soon as we finish each stage. Pete is maintaining steady progress by starting with the early group and keeping to a pace that he can sustain. There is a steely determination building in the group and we are all focussed on getting to the finish – individually and collectively. I have found that a little treat towards the end of the stage provides both CV and me with a good boost. Let me tell you about today's 'little treat'.

Passing through the town of Bloomfield I spotted an ice cream parlour. The car park was quite full which was a good sign. I pulled over to investigate – the rest of the group carried on and I said I would be happy to make my own way to the finish. Looking inside, it was quickly apparent that I had arrived at ice cream heaven. A delicious selection was available, all home-made. CV and I opted for a small pecan maple variety in a cone. I should have sensed trouble when we were told that we might find a bowl and spoon helpful. 'Small' turned out to be three scoops, large scoops by my definition, creating a veritable mountain of ice cream. Taking my spoils outside I found a quiet corner and CV and I began to tuck in. This was ice cream of the highest order. Proper ice cream; rich and creamy with the sweet tangy taste of maple and the slightly salty flavour of pecan. I have to say that it was quite possibly better that the Pecan Fudge Pie that Mary teased me with in Somerset, Kansas. But I imagine she would hold a different view and assert that the pie was better! Whatever, today the sheer quantity of ice cream, our 'small portion', defeated CV and me so we decided that discretion was the better part of valour and reluctantly headed off on the final leg of the day.

Riding on our own gave us the chance to up the speed and burn off the extra calories from our ice cream feast. We were making excellent progress when we had a potentially tour-ending mishap. There are three things, readers, that I dread on tour. Three ways that could force us to abandon. First is getting sick, so we are as scrupulous as we can be about our hygiene, particularly at SAGs when lots of people are handling the same food. I have known riders succumb, leaving them with no choice but to head home. Second, a major mechanical – a bike breaker. And third, serious injury – broken bones, especially collar bones the cyclists Achilles Heel as it were. Well today we had the luckiest of escapes and managed to cheat two of the three threats.

A couple of miles from the finish we were whizzing gently downhill at about 35 miles per hour along a long, wide, smooth shoulder. We were so happy that we were about to burst into song. Our reverie was cut short by an almighty bang and the total and instant loss of air from the rear wheel accompanied by the sound and feel of the rim bumping and grinding on the tarmac. But worse than that, CV who was bearing the brunt of the severe vibration, began to swing from side to side. I spent the next two hundred yards desperately trying to stay upright while reducing our speed. The rear brake was largely ineffective due to the speed and the flat tyre. Using the front brake too harshly risked accentuating the swinging into a jackknife with the near-certain result that we would hit the tarmac hard. Eventually, and still upright, we managed to come to a stop and I unclipped from the pedals and almost fell over because my legs were shaking and weak. As we tried to regain our composure I heard a voice behind me say: "Buddy, are you okay?" or words to that effect. Looking up I saw a Highway Patrolman walking towards me and behind him was his car with the roof lights flashing. Once I had gathered my wits and we had made our introductions I learned that he had seen the blowout happen and quick as a flash he had acted to slow the following traffic in case I veered out onto the carriageway. He remained with us until I had replaced the tube and temporarily boosted the tyre as there was a quarter inch-sized hole in the tyre wall. Then, after shaking my hand and wishing us well on the ride to Boston, he followed us for about half a mile once we got going again. It was a mighty relieved Captain and CV who eventually pulled into our hotel.

All's well that ends well though. I fitted a new rear tyre and a front one as well. I have no idea what caused the blowout. CV has stopped shaking and we were both ready to get going again tomorrow. In my experience the best medicine in these situations, apart from a glass of beer, is to get on with it. So that's precisely what we're going to do. And besides, tomorrow is a stage that I have been eagerly anticipating. As I hope you will discover.

Stage 38: Sunday 24 June, Canandaigua to Syracuse (72 Miles)

After yesterday's excitement CV and I made a pact at our morning team talk. Throttle back and take it a bit easier. Today's stage was one that I had been eagerly anticipating for some time because of a connection to another of my passions. More in a moment. First let me set the scene and deal with the essentials. With low cloud, mist and fog floating around and a cooler temperature, the ride started this morning with what was uncannily like a proper autumnal day. In June? That can't be right. Anyway it was one of those rides inviting the classic 'Do I' or 'Don't I' question. I'm referring to the donning of my rain jacket. I did and then I didn't and then I did again and then I didn't again. OK, you've got it? Fine, I'll shut up about it now

Within five miles guess what happened? A puncture for Emil so just as we had warmed up we had to stop and cool down. We both hoped that this wasn't the start of 'one of those days...' It wasn't as it turned out. By now, fixing punctures is something we take in our stride. After all we've had lots of practice. We were soon up the road and setting a good pace with the help of a modest tailwind. With the fog reducing visibility somewhat it was a day for lights – front and rear. As we ate up the miles we passed through Geneva and then Waterloo. Waterloo was designated as the birthplace of Memorial Day by President Lyndon B Johnson on 26 May, 1966. This year it was celebrated on 28 May when we rode from Las Vegas to Tucumcari on Stage 14. That seems like an eon ago now.

Leaving Waterloo behind we reached Seneca Falls where, I discovered, the first convention on Woman's Rights had been held over two days in 1848. There's a plaque marking the location. The convention was a landmark event marking the start of a movement that grew relentlessly leading in time to the 19th Amendment to the US Constitution which was passed into law in 1920 giving women the right to vote throughout the USA. As we rode through the town I found myself wondering about the pace of change and I was more than a little surprised to subsequently discover that it took over 60 years for all of the remaining states to ratify it, Mississippi being the last to do so, in 1984. Of course, the right to vote is only a part of the story and I have plenty of friends who understandably feel that there is still a way to go. Discovering these little nuggets of history has been one of the most enjoyable aspects of this tour.

Now, earlier on I hinted at my eager anticipation for today's stage. Let me unpack this a bit – hang on in there as it might feel a bit left field. Those who are familiar with my writing will know that I love Bob Dylan. And once again let me emphasise that it's a love of his writing, his lyrics and not any other sort of love. I first tuned into His Bobness through the Basement Tapes and related stuff from The Band ('Music From Big Pink'). What did it for me was the creative inspiration they obtained from the countryside and lifestyle of upstate New York from which they crafted some fabulous music. Now I appreciate that where I was riding today wasn't anywhere near Woodstock or Saugerties but the gentle lifestyles amongst the woods and forests that in part inspired their music has been with me for a long time. Earlier this year I read Robbie Robertson's excellent autobiography, *Testimony*, which rekindled my interest. I was keen today to look much more closely at the character and atmosphere of this part of New York State and to try and find some inspiration of my own. And yes, I was lucky enough to find it.

Long leafy lanes, gently rolling hills, canals, lovely wooden houses – each individually distinctive provided a rich tapestry and backdrop for the ride. A great ride! So rich that at least twice I failed to notice the Garmin telling me to make a turn. This was a very pastoral landscape interspersed with some lovely towns and villages and it was easy, for me at least, to understand how environments like this can fuel such creativity. It's helped me to start making sense of some of the things I have experienced and learned on this extended tour. About my understanding of this great country and its people. After such a short time spent in a relatively small part of this vast nation I know that I have barely scratched the surface. But I have an appetite and a thirst for learning more. And a hope that some of the friendships I have made on this tour will enable me to do just that. But in the meantime I have made a note to return here, perhaps linked to another goal of riding in New England. What I can say for sure is that as I emerged from the woods approaching Syracuse I felt quite rejuvenated. I even had a little sing song of my own – a quick blast of 'This Wheel's on Fire'. (Look it up if you want to know more.) But in the light of yesterday's excitement I shut up pretty quickly – CV's wheel is definitely not on fire!

Stage 39: Monday 25 June, Syracuse to Herkimer (72 Miles)

BBC and the Euros reformed today. Pete, who had been 'resting' by setting off with the earlier group (they're not slower, honestly), applied for re-instatement. So we held a short meeting on the start line and voted (4-1; Bruce how could you!) to let him re-join us. I have to say that I have been missing both his company and his Scottish wit on the road these past few days. Since our first ride to the Hollywood Hills before the tour started, we have travelled a long road together and got to know each other really well. As the only two Brits on the tour we have formed an alliance and have spent a lot of time together – on and off the road. I was delighted to spend a large part of today riding alongside him again and enjoying his company.

Today was much like yesterday, only better. More of the delightful upstate New York countryside on smooth, largely traffic-free county roads. To make the ride even better, the sun was shining and my rain jacket was firmly packed away. Our route has been following the Erie Canal which runs from Buffalo on Lake Erie to Albany on the Hudson River. When construction was completed in 1825 it was the second longest canal (363 miles) in the world. Today it extends for 524 miles. It has played a major role in the commercial activities and economy of the USA. Although a small number of commercial vessels still use it, now it is primarily a recreational resource and has been designated as a National Heritage Corridor. Many of the towpaths running alongside it have been converted into cycle routes, mostly gravel so we had to stay off them. The great thing about following a canal meant that the gradients were likely to be pretty gentle, which at this stage of the tour was no bad thing.

As we rode along on the first part of the stage to the SAG I spent a lot of time looking at and trying to understand the countryside we were passing through. There are lots of trees, woods and forests which gave it a very enclosed feeling. From time to time, where the tree cover had been removed, great sweeping views opened up particularly northwards where I could see rolling hills in the distance. The houses here were a constant source of fascination for me. They come in all shapes and sizes and were mostly constructed from wooden boards. No two houses were the same; each had its own distinctive character. The yards around the houses were usually grassed though not normally on the same scale as I saw in Ohio. The most striking feature was that many, if not most properties have a slightly scruffy and disorderly feel to them which, in my opinion actually enriches and enhances their character. The whole atmosphere of the area was slightly sleepy and laid back.

Interspersed between the solitary houses were some delightful villages. We stopped in once such village, Canastota which is alongside the canal. The name is derived from the Iroquois language – Knisten Stota meaning 'cluster of pines near still waters'. A couple of the bridges and walls have some delightful murals celebrating the canal's heritage and history. But there is much more to the history of the village which I discovered to my delight.

Onion farming has been an important part of the village's economy. The highly fertile silty soil here, known as 'muck', was especially suited for growing vegetables and between 1900 and 1970 Canastota was known as the onion capital of the world. Onion farming was pioneered by Sicilians who settled in the area in the 1890s. The trees growing in the swamps were cleared, often using dynamite, and the land drained. Farms were based on simple shacks with a few outbuildings including a barn and storage for the onions. There was no electricity and wood or coal were used for heating, Water came from wells dug on the land and rainwater was frequently used for clothes washing. Some families also owned winter homes in the nearby village but living on site meant that the farming families could start work as soon as the sun rose each day. Working conditions were harsh involving manual labour and the days were long, often in excess of 12 hours. Whole families, parents and children, worked their enterprises. It was said that children from the muck farming families took their shoes off to work in the wet muddy fields when school ended in the summer and didn't put them back on until going back to school in the autumn. For a variety of reasons including better job opportunities elsewhere, the harsh wet weather and changing agricultural practices, the farms fell into decline during the 1940s and 50s. Today most of the farms are in ruins and the land has become a wet wilderness again.

As we rode through the village I was surprised to see a sign to the International Boxing Hall of Fame. Two world champions, Carmen Basilio and his nephew, Billy Backus are from the village. Each year on the second weekend in June, Canastota hosts an event to induct new members to the Hall of Fame. Past attendees include Muhammad Ali, George Foreman and Joe Frazier. A Sunday parade and an induction ceremony are held to honour past and current Hall of Fame inductees. Professional boxers become eligible for induction five years after their retirement and are chosen by members of the Boxing Writers Association of America and an international panel of boxing historians.

With a relatively short stage, fast roads and a tailwind we made excellent time and were in danger of completing the stage before noon. To ease things a tad when we spotted Dave's Diner we pulled over and had some fantastic ice-cream. Proper ice cream! CV and I plumped for a serving of Sea Salt Caramel in a cup. Recognising the risks of overindulgence from our last feast we opted for the small portion. We both agreed that it was more than sufficient.

Despite this pause we still arrived in Herkimer much earlier than normal. Our hotel, which I christened the Chicken Shed, was, I have to say, underwhelming and at the opposite end of the spectrum from the comparative luxury of the Hampton Inn which we had left a little over six hours earlier. CV and I certainly got close and personal when we subsequently tucked up for the night. Such is life. Every cloud has a silver lining though and Person Number Three, Navi, Pete and I went for a stroll into the town and discovered an excellent little restaurant. I had a wonderful strawberry and spinach salad with nuts, berries and feta cheese. Possibly the best lunch I have enjoyed on the tour to date.

Every so often small events happen spontaneously which add considerably to the fun of the tour. This evening was no exception. As we finished yet another dinner of 'standard fare', this time at an Applebee's outlet, Bruce decreed that we should go in search of ice cream; specifically some of Ben and Jerry's finest. A couple of hundred yards away, across the parking lot, we could see a Walmart store. As Bruce, with his inflamed knee was finding it difficult to walk, we perched him in a shopping cart and with much laughter pushed him across the lot, in the process receiving some comments about adults behaving like children from rather less joyful onlookers. Arriving at the ice cream section we discovered that the Ben and Jerry's cabinet was empty. Never one to be defeated, Person Number Three found a kid stacking shelves and despatched him to the storage area for fresh supplies. After a few minutes and in a scene that was best described as surreal, the kid returned, pushing another shopping cart that was absolutely overflowing with pint tubs of the aforementioned Ben and Jerry's. It seemed that he had loaded up with several tubs of every flavour imaginable. Subsequent research on the Interweb revealed that at any one-time Ben and Jerry's produce between 40 and 50 different varieties. Making our choices and leaving the kid with a good tip we returned to the Chicken Shed to consume the spoils. I wish I could say that I subsequently slept well but sadly not. Here's the thing though. It wasn't a case of being hyperactive on a sugar overdose. It was the noise of the railway on one side of my room and the highway on the other. By the time my cock crowed in the morning I was wide awake. CV on the other hand, slept like a baby.

Stage 40: Tuesday 26 June, Herkimer to Albany (79 Miles)

Waking this morning I received some very sad news that a friend, a Bianchi cousin of mine, Tim Elliot had passed away while out riding his bike. Although we had never met face to face I counted Tim as a friend. Tim was the central figure, the bottom bracket, that drove the Bianchi Owners Club USA forward. I had originally contacted him earlier this year when I was preparing for the tour. From our very first exchange Tim was both extraordinarily helpful and very friendly to me. He was a source of great advice and good humour. But more than that, once I had started the tour Tim frequently sent me messages of support and encouragement which I really appreciated.

As some readers will know I regard fellow Bianchi riders as my extended family and I am proud that I have cousins and uncles all over the world. Whenever we meet (in the UK) our reunions are fantastic occasions. The cousins chat to each other and there is a lot of Passione Celeste around. Judging from the outpouring of comments and memories about Tim that I have seen my US cousins share over the last 24 hours, it is beyond any doubt that Passione Celeste, what I describe as the very DNA of Bianchi, is widespread and heartfelt. So today, I dedicated my ride to my friend and my cousin Tim. And Tim, if you are reading this from afar, I hope you enjoyed the ride too.

Leaving Herkimer this morning there was a distinct chill in the air. So much so that for the first time since we left Los Angeles I was wearing my arm warmers. With a blue sky and sunshine I suspected that it wouldn't be long before they came off and I wasn't wrong. Once again the route followed the Erie Canal and Mohawk River from start to finish. With yet more superb scenery and relatively quiet, smooth roads, the ride was a delight. Like yesterday, much of the ride was under dense tree cover but from time to time clearings and pockets of open farmland created spectacular views across the lush, green land.

The Mohawk River is the largest tributary of the Hudson River and historically has been a strategically important transport corridor through the Appalachian Mountains. It is named after the Mohawk people whose territory once extended from southern Quebec and eastern Ontario, south to New Jersey and east to Vermont. They are known as the Keepers of the Eastern Door who protected the Iroquois Confederation against invasions from the east. The rich supply of flint stones in the area gave them an early economic advantage as they traded the stones, used for tool making, with their neighbours. Following contact with European settlers in the seventeenth century, the population was devastated by an outbreak of smallpox, to which they had no natural resistance. Over time, the fate and fortunes of the Mohawk fluctuated considerably. In more recent times they have played an important role in the development of iron, steel and construction industries, both in New York City and in Quebec. Latterly, and with considerable controversy, there have been moves to develop casinos to encourage more financial independence. Some of these efforts remain subject to legal challenges.

With a relatively short distance to cover we were able to ride at a leisurely pace, stopping regularly to look at the views and take some photos. At our first SAG, after 40 miles, I got chatting to another cyclist who happened to be passing by. In the course of our conversation I found out that he had completed a century ride in every one of the 50 states of the USA. That set me thinking. The logistics of doing this would be quite challenging. I worked out that by the end of the tour I will have ridden a century in four states, not counting the centuries that started in one state and finished in another, which would raise my total to seven. I have also ridden two in Ohio! So, following a strict interpretation I only have 46 states to go. Has a seed been sown?

The European theme of recent days was still present, especially when we reached Amsterdam. First settled by Dutch immigrants in 1710, the area was called Veedersburgh after Albert Veeder an early mill owner. With an influx of settlers from New England the town's name was changed to Amsterdam in 1803. The arrival of the Erie Canal in 1825 created a major economic boost for the town which became well known for the carpets manufactured here. The city was badly damaged by floods caused by Hurricane Irene in 2011. As I rode by today it seemed that the damage had largely been restored. Passing the end of Eagle Street I spotted a roadside sign and discovered that Kirk Douglas, the actor, was born here in 1916. He was the son of Russian emigrant Jews and had six sisters. Times were tough then as he noted in his autobiography:

"My father, who had been a horse trader in Russia, got himself a horse and a small wagon, and became a ragman, buying old rags, pieces of metal, and junk for pennies, nickels, and dimes... Even on Eagle Street, in the poorest section of town, where all the families were struggling, the ragman was on the lowest rung on the ladder. And I was the ragman's son."

Before becoming an actor Kirk had more than forty jobs including selling snacks to mill workers in order to earn money to buy milk and bread for his family. His really was a story of rags to riches.

While we were chatting over breakfast this morning, Pete, who was proud of his Scottish heritage, had mentioned that we would be passing through a town called Scotia. I am not sure quite what he expected to find; he did express a hope for haggis, neeps and tatties but I suspected he was going to be disappointed. (I was proved right.) But in terms of distance and timing it was an ideal spot to stop and enjoy lunch and cold glass of beer. And enjoy it we did as we sat on the terrace of a bar and watched people pass by on their daily routines. Scotia was established by Alexander Lindsay Glen who named it after Scotland, his home country. Historically its main claim to fame was for broom making. In the 1800s over 1 million brooms were produced annually – that's a lot of sweeping! Nowadays it is principally a residential base for people who work in the surrounding area.

We rode the final 15 miles to Albany, the New York State Capital, along some lovely, gently undulating if rather rough roads. As we made our way along I found myself wondering what cousin Tim would have made of today's stage. I rather think he would have liked it. So Tim, rest easy and ride easy. Passione Celeste!

Stage 41: Wednesday 27 June, Albany to Brattleboro (77 Miles)

Our morning route raps have started to become quite comical and the Headteacher is having difficulty holding our attention as end of term fever sets in. This morning several of us were engrossed in watching a video of our great Walmart Ben and Jerry's expedition from a couple of days ago. So absorbed were we that most of the briefing passed over our heads. Literally. But between us we managed to gather most of the essential information that wasn't covered in the day's route sheet. After several stages of comparatively flat riding I was looking forward to today's stage which looked like including some proper hill climbing. At 34 miles the route notes commented: "Begin 6.3-mile climb; last 3.5 steeper." I was quite excited at the prospect, as was CV.

We left the Holiday Inn Express in Albany and crossed over Hudson River before immediately heading upwards. Each day two groups set off at 30 minutes intervals. This helps manage the flow of riders through SAGs and helps with other logistical aspects of each stage. Today, however, the early group arrived at an impassable road closure, a bridge that was being repaired, and had to double back. Consequently, they then met the later group (us) coming up the road so we were now all riding as one. With the possibility of being the leader on the road for once, CV and I wound it up and set off on a little break of our own.

Capitalising on our lead we opted for a short pause at the SAG at 25 miles before continuing on to the day's climb. At the start of the climb we crossed the state line into Vermont (The Green Mountain State and number 13 on the tour). I had been told that Vermont was an exceptionally pretty state so I was looking forward to seeing it. Once over the state line the climb began. Let me just say that it was a real delight. Longish, gentle gradients (always less than 10 per cent), a broad smooth shoulder to ride on and superb views of the densely forested hills I was riding through. I got settled in, dropped onto CV's granny ring and spun my way upwards, tapping out a nice easy rhythm. What a pleasure, what bliss. Especially as it wasn't too hot either. As I climbed steadily upwards on my own I found myself thinking just how lucky I was. Although there have been several challenges, some difficulties and more than a few disappointments along the way the riding has been very fulfilling and rewarding. Today was one of those special days when my head and my heart were soaring free. With only one more full stage left to ride I was determined to make the best of the day and enjoy it as much as I could. Gradually making my way up the climb I almost wished it would never end. The climb lasted just under one hour during which time CV and I ascended about 1,600 feet. With the accumulated mileage in my legs the climbing felt almost effortless. Apart from a few cars I didn't see a single soul. I really enjoyed the peace and the solitude of the ascent, enjoying the scenery that we passed through and I had lots of time to let my mind wander freely as I looked back over past stages of the tour.

Cresting the summit of the Green Mountain, CV and I then enjoyed a long, fast descent which seemed to go on for ever. Some roadworks meant that we had to check our speed a couple of times so we didn't get above 40 miles per hour. Without the roadworks I am sure we could easily have topped 50 miles per hour. But this wasn't the end. Another lesser climb, Hogback Mountain was waiting as a sort of encore for the day. The long descent was pretty good too, marred only by the rough surface which meant we had to pay close attention and pick our riding lines carefully. I was pleased to discover that we have left behind any lingering fears from the blowout incident.

Eventually we arrived at Brattleboro which I had been told was a delightful place and I wasn't disappointed. I managed to find the bike shop to buy a new rear flashing light as my old one seems to have packed up. I spent a very pleasant quarter of an hour chatting to one of the owners, Barbara Walsh, about the tour and cycling generally in Vermont. What she shared with me has left me feeling that I must come back and spend more time here. Indeed, I already have the germ of an idea developing so who knows what might happen.

There is nothing like a bit of inside information to help with finding a good dinner venue. By an amazing coincidence, Mary and Robin who were now enjoying their own tour of New England, had spent the previous night in Brattleboro and recommended the Brattleboro Tavern and said that if I did go there I had to try the sprouts. I discovered that the Tavern was only a short walk away from our hotel so Pete and I, together with Rod, one of the Three Amigos, strolled over there and we were certainly not disappointed. After a bread platter starter with olives, hummus and pickles I opted for a steak with a side of deep-fried Brussels sprouts. I have to say that I was somewhat dubious about ordering the sprouts but Mary had raved about them so I decided to give them a go. And I certainly wasn't disappointed. Instead of the somewhat mushy, fatty vegetable that I thought I might be presented with, the sprouts were beautifully crisp, golden amazingly light.

Now here's a little bit of Brussels Sprout trivia for you. One of the towns near where I live in the UK is Diss, on the south Norfolk border. A couple of years ago I read an article about who eats the most sprouts in the UK and Diss came out on top. Apparently, the people of Diss consumed 1,357,525 sprouts over a twelve-month period giving them the highest per capita consumption. How an earth anyone works out this stuff is almost beyond my comprehension. (Supermarket sales are the measure I gather.) While we're on the subject of sprouts, there are more than 110 different varieties of the little green demons and they can be cooked in more than 9,000 different ways. As this is supposed to be a story about a bike ride across the USA I won't tell you the tale of a guy who, to raise money for charity, once rolled a sprout up to the top of Mount Snowdon in North Wales using only his nose! Anyway, with more than my fair share of Vitamins A and C consumed, to say nothing of the fibre I ingested I should have no excuses for a lacklustre performance tomorrow. Later in my hotel room CV pleaded with me to keep any dietary side effects to myself.

Stage 42: Thursday 28 June, Brattleboro to Burlington (100 Miles)

Today's stage was the last full stage of the tour. Tomorrow was effectively going to be a parade to the finish line. A bit like the Tour de France where the last stage is usually a ceremonial one and not a racing stage. We all lined up together for the penultimate departure. I say 'all' but not quite. Once again the Euros were depleted as Pete had snuck back into the early group. (Was it something we said?) So Barry, Bruce, Person Number Three, Emil and I, plus Peyton were the last to leave Brattleboro.

I should probably explain that Peyton (the kid) was recruited in Champaign, Illinois to provide some extra mechanical support for the tour. He had been working in a bike store there and as far as I could tell was kidnapped – willingly I understand. Bruce and Person Number Three have adopted the role of surrogate parents and have taken him under their wing and have been 'educating' him on the ins and outs of life on tour. Being young he has limitless reserves of energy and his antics on the bike are a constant source of amusement to us. But when all is said and done, his mechanical skills are excellent. He has slotted in very nicely.

The big challenge today was rain. Huge fat drops of the stuff had been falling throughout the night and the road surfaces were glistening, covered in many places with sheets of running water. Elsewhere, there were puddles which hid potentially wheel-buckling and bone-breaking potholes. The leaden grey skies with dense low clouds swirling amongst the treetops all spoke of a very wet day in the saddle. A glance at the weather app on my phone only served to confirm my visual analysis. Today's riding was going to be difficult and would require intense concentration. Having got so tantalisingly close to achieving my EFI, CV and I were going to have to exercise extreme caution.

We rolled down the hill back into Brattleboro and crossed over the Connecticut River before reaching the New Hampshire State line – the fourteenth state on the tour and known as the Granite State because of its extensive quarries. Then it was up into the hills again with some quite testing climbs. Short and sharp but nothing too severe. For a lot of us, the euphoria of nearly reaching the end seems to have added some impetus and strengthened our resolve.

Much of the route was through forested areas, mixtures of conifers and deciduous trees with lots of delightful small villages in between. Unfortunately the road surfaces were quite sketchy which meant that I really had to concentrate on the tarmac in front of me. This was not the time for experiencing a wheel or frame breaking pothole incident – or worse. I have, however, made a mental note that this is an area that would be worth revisiting should the opportunity arise. In fact I would quite like to do a tour around New England, perhaps from Maine down to Connecticut and Rhode Island. I reckon with a bit of planning I might be able to knock out six centuries in a week. Now there's a thought...

For the first 10 miles or so I was entirely preoccupied with the weather and engaged in a mental battle to conqueror my feelings about the rain. I was so focussed on pushing on through the rain that I paid little attention to my surroundings. At one point I was aware that Bruce, who was a couple of hundred yards ahead of me had pulled off the road. Normally, I would follow suit. But with today's rain, a glance at my Garmin showed the road proceeding straight ahead so I carried on, passing by Bruce. About a mile of so further along I realised why he had pulled over. He had spotted one of New Hampshire's famous covered bridges and wanted to grab a photo of it. I cursed loudly because when doing my pre-tour research I had made a note to do the same. One of my all-time favourite films is 'The Bridges *of Madison County*' and while it is set in Iowa the shots of the bridges have always captivated me. The chance to see a covered bridge up close was one that I didn't want to miss. I actually stopped and considered turning around but in the end the weather won out and I decided to keep riding. At their peak there were once around 10,000 covered bridges across the USA. Now only about 750 remain; apparently half of the world's total.

After about 15 miles we passed through the small town of Winchester which was established in the first part of the eighteenth century and was named after the Marquess of Winchester. The town was where Graves and Company, one of America's first musical instrument manufacturers opened here soon after the town's founding and made a range of brass and woodwind instruments

As we progressed eastwards the roads gradually got busier and we received a few suggestions from lippy motorists who clearly didn't appreciate sharing 'their' tarmac with us. Added to the sketchy surfaces it meant we had to concentrate even more. This was one of the few occasions where I felt that I actually needed my rear-view mirror. Thus far it has largely been a convenience. Not having to look back over my shoulder this morning meant that I could stay fully focussed on the road in front of me.

Arriving at the first SAG of the day I found Pete was still there so we decided to continue onwards together. It was great to be reunited with him again. All of a sudden up popped the Massachusetts state line. So suddenly that we almost missed it and had to turn around to get the photo for the collection. So that's it, the last state of the tour, number 15. Quite a landmark really. Unlike 13 of the other states we have passed through, Massachusetts, is actually a commonwealth. But the distinction is a subtle one with its roots in history. In the late 18th century constitutional writers sometimes used the word 'commonwealth' in the legal documents that established a state. Around this time the term was used to describe groups of people who made up a nation or state. Commonwealths are states but states are not commonwealths. And for the record, the other commonwealth that we rode through was Pennsylvania. Massachusetts is known as the Bay State and in some circles as the Baked Bean State after the Baked Navy Bean, which in 1993 was designated as the State's official bean. Now there's a thing!

As we approached Burlington, Bruce came alongside me and asked if I would be interested in doing a few extra miles at the end to turn today's stage into a century ride. Well, it didn't take much asking – another century. The Captain wouldn't miss out on that. So that's exactly what we did. We arrived at the stage finish and then turned around and did another seven miles to take us over the hundred. Ironically, as we rode away from the hotel forecourt the ferocity of the rain increased. It was now so heavy that I could barely see the road ahead of my front wheel. Throwing caution to the wind we backtracked the day's route and then rode around a housing estate to ensure we completed the requisite miles. What a great way to mark the end of the tour!

Stage 43: Friday 29 June, Burlington to Revere Beach (17 Miles)

Before starting today's stage some long overdue and important business had to be concluded. Back on the 2nd June on the stage from Dodge City to Great Bend you might remember that I won a bet with Bruce by not telling the story of Pawnee Rock, situated nearby. So today Bruce paid his dues and I got my £1 and €1. Person Number Three acted as the official witness. Well actually I got £2 which is okay, Bruce, as we're apparently leaving the European Union so the €1 would probably not be much use to me. And in the unlikely event that anyone is still wondering about the story of Pawnee Rock I can spill the beans now that I have trousered my winnings. And that seems entirely appropriate as we are in The Baked Bean State.

Pawnee Rock is a famous landmark on the historic Santa Fe trail. Strategically it was an important viewpoint where Indian tribes used it to pinpoint approaching buffalo herds and wagon trains. For some it was regarded as the most dangerous place on the Santa Fe trail. For others it was a waypoint denoting that about half of the journey westwards was complete. Over the years many of the people passing by carved their names into the soft rock. Sadly by the 1870s much of the rock had been removed to be used as building stone. Since 1970 it has been officially protected and listed in the National Register of Historic Places. So there you are. That's what I didn't tell you about before in order to win the bet!

Today's stage was effectively a parade lap to the beach. Just a few short miles to mark the crossing of a continent. Just as we did on the first day of the tour in El Segundo, we gathered in front of the hotel in Burlington and set off in groups of three. Pete, Emil and I, previously The Fabs and now the Euros, lined up alongside each other and then off we went. With such a lot that has happened I was feeling very emotional. The euphoria of actually completing the ride – 3,400 Miles and achieving EFI Status. A realisation that I would almost certainly never ride with this whole group of wonderful people again but a hope that some of us may cross paths again one day. And some sadness too that it was not possible for Mary, who has become close to me, to be there as I crossed the finishing line and share in my achievement.

We rode southeast from Burlington gradually crossing Boston's suburbs before we all stopped to group up again and get ready for the final procession to Revere Beach. We were formed into a line in pairs and I was both pleased and very proud to be standing next to Pete. We recalled our first ride together, to the Hollywood Hills, before the tour started. We have travelled over so much ground together since, both on the tarmac and off it, and we have become good friends. But more than that, there is a bond between us that I know we will always share. I look forward to the day when we ride together again.

Taking advantage of the brief halt, I asked Pete to hold my bike and went to the front of the line and worked my way back saying 'goodbye' to each of the riders individually. Fellow riders and kindred spirits most of whom I have ridden with for at least a few miles and got to know well together with a few others who I now wished I knew a bit better. Such is life on a Tour. From every one of my fellow riders I have drawn tremendous inspiration. Each of us, experienced cyclists or not, has shared a unique experience and overcome so many obstacles and challenges that threatened our achievements. I will treasure those memories forever. A good route makes a good ride or tour. And great tours are made by great people. This has been one of the greatest tour teams I have ever ridden with.

We were led in convoy, with a police escort, along the final four miles to Revere Beach. We must have looked a splendid sight as so many passersby stopped to gaze at us. We even received some cheers from the sidewalk and several car horn toots. Then suddenly we turned the last corner and in front of us there was the Atlantic Ocean; journey's end. The sea front was lined with people, families and friends who had come to cheer and congratulate their riders. There was quite a party atmosphere. Then everyone gathered round as we dipped our wheels in the ocean and posed for a last group photograph.

I had one final act to perform. When we left Manhattan Beach on 13 May I had picked up a small pebble from the beach. It had been in the back pocket of my jersey every day since. It has been a constant companion for me and CV throughout the tour. Each morning it has sat in front of us at our one-to-one meetings in our hotel room as a daily focus for collecting our thoughts and getting ready to ride. I spent a couple of minutes standing on Revere Beach silently contemplating what had happened to us; to CV my constant companion, and me, over the last seven weeks. Then drawing my arm behind me I threw the pebble as far as I could into the Atlantic Ocean. We were both happy to see it fly and sad to let it go. We have travelled a long way together. We have travelled over 3,400 miles or 215 million inches and achieved our EFI!

9. CAN I TELL YOU SOMETHING?

It's late in the evening on 5 July and I am sitting at 40,000 feet somewhere over the Atlantic Ocean. I am on my way home. I have been looking back at the last few days which have been quite eventful. The day after the tour ended was a sad one for me as I said my goodbyes to Pete who had been my constant companion since we first rode together to the Hollywood Hills nearly two months ago. We have shared so much together and I hope that one day we will be able to ride together again.

Rather than mooch around the hotel and at Pete's suggestion CV and I went out for a ride. It was quite a strange feeling to ride without a purpose, other than for its own sake. After spending two months riding daily towards a destination following a fixed route the concept of simply riding around randomly for a couple of hours was almost unsettling. I remember reading an article about musicians who, having given a successful concert or after completing a tour, found it very difficult to get back down to earth and the realities of 'normal' daily life. Now I had a better understanding of what they felt.

Once the tour was over I spent a few days exploring Boston and taking in the sights. I also enjoyed a great reunion with Mary who, having completed her tour of New England with Robin, was in the city with her son, Jack, for a couple of days. I spent a memorable 4th of July in the city and basked in the party atmosphere. I particularly enjoyed following the Freedom Trail, a walk that was distinctively marked by a red brick line set into the pavements which was originally established in 1951. The route took me past numerous historically significant sites telling

Boston's history over the last 250 years and role the city has played since the American Revolution. As one of my goals for undertaking the tour was to learn about America and its people, this was a perfect way to conclude my quest. One lesson I have learnt though, is that I have barely scratched the surface of this great nation. It has certainly given me an appetite for returning and learning more.

As my flight headed ever eastwards my mind travelled back over the tour as I thought about some of the places I visited, the people I met and the rides I have experienced. I tried to make sense of what has certainly been both an exciting and also a challenging ride. Riding a big tour like this had left me feeling cocooned from the outside world. It was a bit like being in a bubble which had been relentlessly rolling forward eastwards, incessantly clocking up mile after mile. It has been a strange sensation. I was always in and connected to the real world, yet in many ways I felt disconnected from it. Almost like a spectator gazing down on a nation and its people.

I cast my mind back over the riding. Some of it was hard, very hard indeed. The western deserts of California, Arizona and New Mexico with their intense heat. More heat in the east with the addition of high humidity. Lots of interstate highway riding too, none of it particularly fulfilling yet, in the absence of other roads, the only way to cover the ground in a reasonable span of time. I recalled how riding on the interstates brought us together, a disparate group of riders most of whom didn't know each other at the start of the tour, to form a team of mutually supportive friends. The deep bonds we formed while helping each other to change tubes following the numerous punctures we all experienced. In one afternoon I had more punctures than I had in all my rides over the previous three years. I heard that the groups' puncture count that day was over 40! But over dinner that same evening, many of us were sharing our stories and laughing at what otherwise would have been a pretty miserable experience. There was a level of understanding and empathy between us that I have rarely felt on other tours.

The riding itself was certainly challenging and demanding but the landscapes we rode through and the splendour and the diversity of the scenery we experienced, added to and enhanced my riding experience. To take one example from many, the stage from Prescott to Flagstaff was stunning. Truly stunning. The low, distant line of red, weather-worn rocks which slowly transformed into a seemingly impenetrable wall as I approached it and then the surprise of a cleft, a narrow canyon providing an escape route up and out. The exhilaration of riding upwards through the hairpin bends to the top, all while inhaling the almost intoxicating aroma of the Ponderosa Pine resin was stunning. And the realisation that I was surrounded by a landscape that was at least 200,000 years old was humbling. The raw splendour of this landscape did as much to raise my heart rate as the climb itself.

The harsh landscapes of the western deserts and mountains contrasted markedly with the softer, more manicured and managed landscapes of the east – in Ohio and New Hampshire for example. As I rode eastwards, and especially along the old Route 66, I was moved by what I saw – a battle between humans and nature. In the west, nature appeared to be winning the struggle. I passed by a lot of abandoned properties; homes where the people had struggled to scratch a living from the land and had eventually given up in despair. Old cars and trucks lay abandoned in many of the yards, their ages providing clues as to how long ago, or how recently, the end had come for the people who once lived here. This was a harsh land where it appeared that survival was inextricably linked to the availability of water. In some places I could see abandoned farms and homes literally slowly dissolving back into the sand.

Further east humans seemed to be on the front foot. More intensive farming, irrigation, a greater population density and more infrastructure. There was much more greenery in the fields, hedgerows, woods and forests. This was softer countryside, almost seeming manicured in Ohio, though New York State had a greater, and to my eye, a more aesthetically pleasing 'couldn't care less' look. Managed certainly, but with an element of randomness and spontaneity which made the scenery more stimulating

In between were the extensive cattle lands of Texas which we rode across briefly. The scale and intensity of the cattle farming that I saw was breath-taking. The sight of the forlorn cattle standing in pens waiting their fate was haunting and an image that remained imprinted on my mind for several days. Similarly, the green maize and soya fields of Indiana served to remind me how much land the human race needs to feed itself. Now, when I eat a barbequed ear of sweetcorn I can't help thinking of those vast fields that stretched to the distant horizons in every direction.

We enjoyed incredibly good weather. By my count we had had about two and a half days of rain. I only needed to wear my rain jacket on two stages. The winds mostly blew in our favour too. Tailwinds that enabled us to roll along at a good pace and on one stage I set a personal best for 10 miles (22 minutes, equivalent to about 27 mph). On only one day did we have to ride into strong headwinds and on a couple of others we had to contend with harsh, gusting sidewinds. Had we faced more headwinds this tour would have been so very different.

The long straight roads became quite a mental challenge. To pass the time I sometimes played what I called the Garmin Game. I would pick out an object the distant horizon, like a water tower and guess how far away it is. Then I looked at my present mileage and tried to avoid looking at the Garmin again until I reached the object I had selected. I regularly underestimated the distances – often by several miles. So, in addition to the physical challenges, the mental challenges were also quite a factor.

The sheer scale of America was a revelation. I always knew I would be in a big country, but I never understood just how big. Individual states here are bigger than the whole of the UK. That, for me, added a totally new dimension to the riding. Riding in the desert was a humbling and occasionally unsettling experience, which as I passed through it, a tiny speck on a massive canvas, made me feel quite insignificant. The same was true when we rode through the maize and soya fields of Indiana and Illinois. The crops stretched away to the horizon uninterrupted for miles in every direction. The flat lands with few opportunities to get higher up made it very difficult to gauge the scale of what I was passing through. More than once I felt like I was afloat in a small dinghy on a vast ocean.

One of my reasons for undertaking the tour was to use it as a means of exploring this great nation. By riding east across the country from Los Angeles to Boston I thought I would gain a great insight into the country. Looking at my road atlas when I returned home and from the many conversations with my fellow tour riders I realised just how little I had actually seen. I had barely scratched the surface. My mind has turned to thoughts of a northern crossing, from say Portland in Oregon to Portland in Maine. Or a southern crossing from Los Angeles to Jacksonville in Florida. Then there are the east and west coasts. And not forgetting the achievements of that rider I met in upstate New York who has ridden a century in every state. The possibilities are limitless and sadly, but realistically, almost certainly beyond me. This tour, this introduction to America, has given me an appetite to see more. I shall return!

With a few notable exceptions I was unprepared for the positive and welcoming reception I received from the people I met along the way. I have always found American people to mostly be very polite: "You're welcome" and "Have a nice day" being the catchphrases that, probably wrongly, have characterised the nation's people in many visitors' minds. In many cases these responses seemed, in my experience to be automatic and somewhat robotic. What surprised me on the tour was the sincerity and interest that I encountered with the people I met. If you are ever looking for a tactic to break the ice with strangers I can wholeheartedly recommend the sweaty lycra approach! It worked for me – every time. Throw in a British accent and success is almost certainly guaranteed. Here's how it goes.

Arriving at a store or a gas station I would find somewhere to prop up my bike. Then after removing my helmet, skully and mitts and giving my face a quick wipe with a flannel that I always carry in my back pocket, I would enter the establishment concerned and have a quick look around. Locate the cold drinks – chocolate milk was always welcome – for the protein. Where was the restroom and was it locked? Did I need to ask for a key? Were there other people in the store? By this time my 'arrival' had usually been noticed by everyone in the store and I was being given the once over. And not always discretely either. Pretty soon thereafter I would usually be engrossed in a conversation. Mostly about me, where I had come from and where I was going. But I also found people were very happy to answer my questions. And I ask a lot of questions! It would have been very easy and often tempting to stay and chat for a good while but as I was always conscious of the need to make progress I rarely had the time to spend more than a few minutes with my new 'best friends'. Wherever possible I plugged my blog and I saw from the Interweb data that I picked up quite a few followers this way. Several people subsequently messaged me as well, referencing our conversations earlier in the day and giving me their good wishes. So, if anyone who joined me on the virtual tour is reading this book, then I would just like to say: "Thank you for your interest, friendship and support. It really did enrich my rides." Even casual encounters at the roadside, for example when I was snagging a photo, passing drivers, especially in the countryside, would often stop to check that I was okay. That inevitably led to a conversation. Oh, the kindness of strangers.

One of the things I found tough was the constant succession of one-night stays. I rarely managed to properly unpack and I lived out of my two kitbags for the duration of the tour. Over the seven weeks of the tour this became quite wearisome. I longed to spend more than two nights in the same bed and had to wait until the end of the tour to achieve this. The constant succession of Hiltons, Holiday Inns, Best Westerns and so on, all built to the same basic formula were largely functional, as they needed to be. How I longed for the occasional room where the floorboards creaked, the wardrobe doors and drawers didn't quite shut and the furniture bore the marks, the chips, dents and scratches of age and longevity. If this sounds odd what I yearned for was bit more character. Character born of quirks and the less than perfect. But the upside of these concrete temples was uniformity and the lack of unwelcome surprises. The air conditioning almost always worked, the Interweb connections were generally easily made. The beds were spacious and comfortable more often than not. And the edge of town locations meant they were usually easy to find at the end of each day's stage. Unfortunately, the downside was that I rarely got an opportunity to explore and learn more about the cities and towns where we were overnighting. The rest days by contrast, with two nights in situ, were wonderful and I had memorable times in Santa Fe, Abilene, Champaign and Erie.

Probably the biggest domestic challenge for me was the food on offer. I guess that my previous tours in Europe, with locally sourced fresh and healthy ingredients cooked to order, have spoilt me. I found breakfasts in the concrete hotels particularly challenging. They were more often a case of providing fuel rather than anything more appetising. I have now eaten enough powered scrambled egg to last the rest of my lifetime! How I longed for wholemeal bread, or a croissant that was still warm from the oven.

While this was never intended to be a gastronomic tour, in my experience the availability of food that I want to eat, rather than food that I have to eat is one of the best morale boosters there is for lengthy tours. Evening meals, when there were several menu options, were usually less challenging but nevertheless often more functional than taste-bud-tempting or mouth-watering. I grabbed the few opportunities to eat out at independent restaurants with gusto and jumped at the chance to eat some 'proper food'. Food that was specifically cooked to order. And especially when there was the chance to chat to the table waiters about the provenance and preparation of the menu choices. Sadly, these were not as frequent as I would have wished.

Underpinning the tour was a support system intended to ensure that we could focus on our riding as much as possible. One of the big factors in my choosing to do the tour with CrossRoads Cycling was their promise of good backup. Although this appeared to be the case at the start and there were eight people listed on the contacts sheet, things degenerated as the tour progressed leading one rider to describe us as participants in a failing experiment. One of the support crew, who I never actually met, 'disappeared' in the first few days. To lose one crew member over seven weeks was understandable and perhaps to be expected. To lose virtually the whole support team suggested that something more fundamental was happening.

Bizarrely, the tour crew seemed to be airbrushed out of our script by the tour company owners, never to be seen of or spoken about by them again. Even more strangely since my riding friends had nothing but praise for the 'lost' crew members and their empathy with us. What this did mean was that as the tour progressed eastwards the level of support dropped significantly and, in my view, below safe levels in some cases. Even during early stages of the tour, the support was variable. Our hot afternoon in the Arizona desert at Hope was a case in point. Without the kind help and water provided by some random passers-by we would have been in some difficulty. Another example of the kindness of the strangers we encountered along the way.

As the tour progressed I found that one day blurred into the next. So much so that I had difficulty sometimes remembering my geography. My encounter with Bridget and her friend in the gas station in New Berlin provided a graphic illustration of this. But we overcame my memory deficiency and enjoyed some great conversation. Thereafter, before going into any store I always had a quick look at the day's cue sheet to make sure that I knew the names of the day's start and end points!

Leaving aside the interstate riding, most of the stages were on good well-surfaced roads with not too much traffic. This meant that I was able to take in a lot of the scenery that I passed through. Most of the stages had their own rewards too. The stage from Chillicothe to Kirksville in Missouri with the 148 rollers was outstanding. Very hard and very hot but also very rewarding. Reaching the top of each crest and looking down before descending to start the next steep ascent was very satisfying. It got quite exciting seeing how fast I could go downhill and then how far up the next rise my momentum would carry me. The stage from Abilene to Topeka in Kansas that I rode with Robin, one of the tour crew, who was inexplicably airbrushed out of the tour the very next day, was pure pleasure – just a perfect day in the saddle. One of the high points of the tour too.

CV, whose full name is Celeste Victoria, was a total delight and the perfect companion for the tour. Together we shared a lot and suffered too; CV in silence. Readers who are familiar with my writings will know all of my Bianchi's have personalities and names. I spend a lot of time in their company and we have a unique relationship. I won't try to explain that here – if you want to know more then read my book, *Passione Celeste*. Suffice to say that I regard them as my second family. CV rose to the challenge of our tour magnificently and despite having to cope with some punishing conditions she breezed through admirably. There was only one issue with her hydraulic brakes which was more of a design fault than a performance issue. She has been a great companion for me. Our one-to-one conversations in our hotel room immediately before the start of each stage, provided great comfort and helped us to clear our minds and ready ourselves for whatever lay ahead.

What really made this tour special was the people I met, especially my fellow riders and the tour support team. Our team of riders was a very diverse group covering a wide age range from mid-twenties to mid-seventies with a great range of experience. Whatever our individual motivations for taking part in the tour, we all shared the delights and the sense of freedom that cycling on the open road enabled us to have. Within a very short time it seemed as if we were one large extended family who had gathered together for a reunion. As one of three overseas riders on the tour I was touched by the way my American counterparts welcomed me into their fold and the information and explanations they willingly shared with me over the seven weeks of the tour. Everything from information about the places we passed through and their history to unveiling the mysteries of some of the food we consumed.

Although over the first few days we naturally formed into smaller groups there was no sense of being better than some or not as good as others. I really enjoyed the times when we were all together – at SAGs or dinners when there were opportunities to chat over the past day's ride and look forward to the next day. All carried out with lots of good-hearted banter and ribbing. The levels of chatter and laughter at these times were the best measure of our enjoyment. And on the few occasions when we were a bit subdued I did a little dance to raise the spirits. It never failed me. Well I don't think it did!

I have made a lot of friendships that I hope will endure, even if only virtually over social media. Pete and I, the two UK members, met and rode together before the tour started and virtually every day thereafter. By the end of the tour he felt almost like a brother. Emil and David who made up The Fab Four during the formative stages of the tour, were great companions. As was Greg who joined us along the way. Emil was with us to the very end in Boston and I felt a big lump in my throat and tears in my eyes when Pete, Emil and I stood together for a final photograph before riding the last 17 miles to Revere Beach. And there is one very special friendship which has defied all the odds, including airbrushing, and which I am particularly excited about for the future. Good rides need good routes. Great rides need great people. It would be an honour and a privilege to ride with any of these people again. But only with a different organisation.

Somewhere over the mid-Atlantic the lights in the cabin were dimmed and I closed my eyes in the hope of getting a few hours' sleep before we landed in London. My last thought as I drifted off was the question Mary almost invariably asked me each day we spoke: "How was your ride?"

Well Mary, can I tell you something?

ACKNOWLEDGEMENTS

This is my story of my tour. I couldn't have done it without the help of a lot of people. I would like to take this opportunity to acknowledge their support and encouragement. And if I have overlooked anyone then that is entirely my fault.

First and foremost, I want to pay tribute to the great people; my fellow riders and the tour crew, who made this a great ride. I have thought long and hard about whether or not to distinguish between the riders who achieved EFI and those who did not. Whether to distinguish between those who undertook the whole tour and those who rode part of it. And finally, whether or not to distinguish the riders from the tour crew. I have decided to make no such distinctions. From where I sat in my saddle, all of these people helped me to achieve my tour, however great or small the part that they played. So, my heart-felt thanks go out to:

Adam Abram, Mark and Susan Chichester, Mary Durkin, Chris Edgerton, Rod Erin, Bruce Goldberg, John Gussenhoven, Bruce Green, Kenneth Ho, Phillip Hawkins, Peyton Kaiser, Don Kieffer, David Kleban, Lawrence Liang, Louis McCray, Bob Mountz, Robin Naismith, Olga Nieves and Diane Witek, Greg Phillips, Robert Pendley, Navi Ramireddy, Barry Roberson, Mike Ruane, Michael Sheskey, Emil and Eve Steiner, Cathy Switzer, Michael Taylor, Tom Thorsteinson, Terry Whitehouse, Pete Wilson, Steve Warner and Ichiro Yamaoda.

I would be honoured to ride with each and any of you again.

I met many wonderful people on the road. The information they provided, the knowledge they shared, always freely given and almost invariably with some good humour thrown in, greatly enriched my tour. The kindness of strangers was almost overwhelming at times. And to all the people who cheered me on my way, through social media, by email and the power of positive thought you provided a hearty diet of energy, encouragement and love for me to thrive on.

Mick Madgett and his team at Madgetts Cycles back home in Diss, Norfolk did a fine job as CV's midwives. She has grown to be a fine lady indeed. Yet again you have delivered the 'goods' and then some.

Production of this book that you are holding would not have been possible without the support of the team at Troubador Publishing. Their patience, perseverance and professionalism ensured that I crossed the finishing line. My friend Barry Lowenhoff took a rather vague brief and created a cover that captured the essence of my tour.

Last, but by no means least, Ziggy kept me moving whenever I showed signs of lollygagging with my writing.